Prodigal Sons and Material Girls

Prodigal Sons and Material Girls
How Not to Be Your Child's ATM

Nathan Dungan

WILEY

John Wiley & Sons, Inc.

Library of Congress Cataloging-in-Publication Data:

Dungan, Nathan, 1965–
    Prodigal sons and material girls : how not to be your child's atm /
By Nathan Dungan.
      p. cm.
    ISBN 0-471-25069-4 (CLOTH : alk. paper)
    1. Parents—Finance, Personal. 2. Children—Finance, Personal.
3. Teenagers—Finance, Personal. 4. Finance, Personal. I. Title.
HG179 .D857 2003
332.024'0431—dc21

                                     2002014014

For my grandparents,
Edith and Orval Dungan and
Jacob and Elizabeth Hansen,
who transferred their values of generosity
to generations present and future.
Their ability to respond to the needs of others
when they had so little
will forever serve as an inspiration.

*"The test of our progress is not whether we add
more to the abundance of those who have much; it
is whether we provide enough for those who have
too little."*

—Franklin D. Roosevelt
(Second Inaugural Address)

Contents

Contents

Foreword

Today's parents have so many responsibilities it is difficult to name them all. Providing basic food and shelter is important, of course, but then so is making sure your child gets a good education and feels loved. Teaching your children to get along with others is critical, and so is showing them how to be independent. Helping a child to understand the dangers of the world is essential, but so is shielding him or her from those dangers.

If you wanted to write down all of the duties of parenthood you'd need a lot of paper and a long afternoon. When you finished, every item on your list would just be a specific version of one general principle: The basic responsibility for all parents is to take care of their children.

In a way, today's parents are no different from parents in the past—both have been given the task of taking care of their children—but in another way today's parents have a very different job from parents in the past. The job of parenting is constantly evolving because we have to redefine "caring" to keep pace with a changing world.

A hundred years ago, for example, caring parents had to be vigilant about their children catching a cold lest it turn into pneumonia. In that era, pneumonia was the leading cause of death among children. Today, thanks to antibiotics we don't live in the same mortal fear of pneumonia. Although parents still try to keep their kids from becoming ill, constant fear of pneumonia no longer concerns most parents.

It's tempting to think that modern knowledge and technology have made the job of taking care of children easier, and in some ways that is exactly what has happened. Parents today do not have to worry as much about many of the challenges that parents faced in the past. Of course, new knowledge and technology have also created new challenges, and so the job of taking care of kids, while different, requires just as much effort and care as it always has.

One of the new challenges for today's parents is the increased competition for the hearts and minds of their children. Our media-saturated world is filled with messages, products, and ideas that are not always in keeping with every parent's values. And making matters more difficult still, the business models of many companies include aggressive targeting of children. The power of Madison Avenue advertising has been brought to bear on young people like never before, so it shouldn't come as a surprise that advertising teaches values to children more effectively than anything else, including family, school, and religion.

It's true that not only does advertising teach values to kids by enticing them with exciting messages and themes, but the sheer amount of advertising kids see is enough to make commercial messages be stiff competition for parents. Media vehicles for advertising like TV, movies, video games, the Internet, radio, and magazines surround kids and bombard them with messages. When you factor in the ads on cereal boxes, packages, and signs you can begin to see how it's possible that children see 1.2 million advertisements each year. Today's children get more information from entities trying to sell something to them than they do from anywhere else.

The creativity, strategy, technology, and more than $230 billion per year from Madison Avenue can be very persuasive for children. The fact is, most children 6 and under do not understand the difference between entertainment and advertisement and cannot distinguish reality from fantasy. In a recent study young children were asked what they would be more likely to believe: something that their parents said was true or something just the opposite that a TV character said was true. Seven out of 10 kids surveyed said they would believe the TV character. The mind of a child is the perfect clean slate for targeted advertising messages.

Advertisers don't just target kids because kids pay attention to ads—advertisers target children because they spend money, a lot of money. Young people 18 and under spend $150 billion in the United States annually, and because more and more parents are at work than ever before, much of this money is being spent without parental supervision. And the amount of money that kids influence their parents to spend is a lot bigger—five times bigger! It's impossible to say why all of that $750 billion is spent, but it's safe to say that many purchases begin with a child saying something like, *"Pleeease can we get this, Mom?"*

The huge amount of money advertisers can get directly and indirectly from young people is the reason automobile manufacturers place ads in children's magazines. It is also the reason kids care what kind of dishwashing soap their parents buy. With all that money at stake, and a track record of success in getting it, you can see why advertisers try to establish brand loyalty by the age of 3. And the high stakes of targeting children is the reason behind yet another phenomenon: a generation of kids whose attitude is "Gotta have it. Gotta have it now." With so much effort on the part of advertisers directed toward urging children to buy on impulse, is it any wonder that the current generation of kids is plagued by a lack of money management skills?

The media age has many benefits for parents and children. The opportunities for education are beyond anything imaginable only a few decades ago, and as part of an influential demographic, children can play an important role in what is being offered in the marketplace. But there is a downside to the spread of commercial messages into so many parts of life as well. Many kids have become hyperconsumers who do not have any idea how to manage money. Perhaps even more alarmingly, a number of experts are seeing a generation of kids who have no understanding of how and why to delay gratification.

In other words, one of the most important challenges parents now face is the fact that most kids don't understand money. And making matters worse, advertisers know kids do not handle money well, and they are quick to take advantage. The good news is that with the help of this book, you can level the playing field with the advertisers. Your children don't have to have trouble with money.

Prodigal Sons and Material Girls: How Not to Be Your Child's ATM shows just how prevalent the problem is. But unlike pneumonia a century ago, it is a problem that many parents may have in their own home without knowing it. The facts and statistics in this book demonstrate the breadth of the problem as well as the particular ways that a lack of money understanding can cause other problems.

In my work I speak with thousands of parents and teachers every year. Many times they are aware of the challenges they face and grateful when someone else seems to understand what they are facing. However, what they really want is help in dealing with the problems. That's where I

think this book is strongest—in giving parents the knowledge and the tools they need to level the playing field. With
Nathan Dungan's help you can compete with Madison Avenue and the other forces that encourage your kids to take
great interest in what money can get them and little interest
in how it does that.

Taking care of children sometimes entails caring
enough to take them away from what they want to do most.
It's easy for kids to want to spend lavishly without any
thought for the cost because there is a lot of pressure on
them to do so. But with the help of the knowledge and tools
in this book you can help your children become, in
Nathan's words, "savvy consumers who make decisions
based on their values." And then you won't have to take
care of your kids when it comes to money, because they'll
take care of themselves.

David Walsh, Ph.D.
President and Founder
National Institute on Media and the Family
Minneapolis, Minnesota

Acknowledgments

I am indebted and grateful to all those who helped make this book possible. I apologize in advance for any omissions.

To my parents, Hildred and Al Dungan, who shaped my financial habits and values early on and instilled in me the joy of using money from a share, save, and spend perspective. Your wisdom and simple philosophy were the seeds for this book. Thank you also for teaching me that the person is greater than the sum of his or her possessions.

To my siblings, Kris, Eric, and Kari, whose encouragement and role modeling was just what their younger brother needed. A very special thank-you to Eric, my computer/technology mentor, for "talking me off the ledge" when my laptop wasn't cooperating. Your patience and wise counsel were there morning, noon, and night.

To Jon Holten, my talented and patient Minneapolis editor, who helped me develop a joy for writing. Thank you for mentoring a first-time author. Not only did you enthusiastically embrace the vision of this book, but you did an artful job of helping me transfer the ideas to the written word.

To my friends in Pennsylvania, who provided input, support, and encouragement as the share, save, and spend concepts first came to life. While there are too many to name, I especially want to thank Sally Kolesar, Rev. Mark Wimmer, Barbara Piston, Debbie Detweiler, and the three Rev. Bobs—Mitman, Hyson, and Linders—for providing me with forums to engage young people and their parents in conversations about money. Those early interactions were the springboard that propelled me on this journey.

To Kathleen Janasz, who "got it" early on and then shared her editorial talent and ideas along the way. Your insight and intuition were tremendous attributes. Thank you for continually challenging me about the focus of the book. Thanks also to her kids for being patient while Mom reviewed the manuscript.

To Debby Englander, my executive editor at John Wiley & Sons, who enthusiastically embraced the project from day one and who patiently tolerated my questions along the way. To Elke Villa, the marketing manager at Wiley, who welcomed the many marketing suggestions with enthusiasm. And to Greg Friedman, Debby's assistant, who skillfully guided me through the technical nuances of writing the book.

To Rev. Loren Mead, a wonderful mentor and friend. Your musings and writing on money were a significant source of inspiration for this book. I especially enjoyed traveling with you on our speaking tour in the fall of 1999. Thank you also for reminding me that when choosing a career path there are several right answers.

To all my friends at Lutheran Brotherhood (now known as Thrivent Financial for Lutherans). If I name one person, I fear I will omit another. So instead let me offer a group thank-you. While it's great to have an idea, this book is living proof that "the whole is greater than the sum of the parts." Thank you for trying something new and embracing the notion that teaching young people about money requires a long-term commitment. From the financial associates throughout the United States to the home office folks in Minneapolis, I truly appreciate the multitude of suggestions and ideas along the way. Because of you, I know this book is stronger.

And finally to Sissy, who has been my Rock of Gibraltar through a sea of change. Your patience and support throughout this transition have been gifts beyond comprehension.

Introduction

The seed for this book was planted back in 1990. At the time, I was a financial adviser living outside Philadelphia, Pennsylvania, when Sally, a religious educator, approached me with a problem and an opportunity she had observed over the last few years. Problem: The increasing consumer pressure directed at young people was overtaking their financial habits and values. Opportunity: Use my skills as a financial services professional to create a workshop that would offer a counter-rhythm—also known as financial balance—to this disturbing trend.

I was intrigued and agreed to help her out.

While doing research for the workshop, I kept thinking about who or what had the greatest impact on how I used money. Without question, the dominant influence on my financial habits and values was my parents. Whether it was learning how to live within my means, helping to learn from my mistakes, saving for a goal, or sharing with a cause, my parents had a hand in shaping my attitude about finances. And as you will read in the book, that is true for the majority of Americans: Parents play *the* greatest role in teaching young people about money—or not.

As I finished writing that first workshop—"Parents, Kids & Money"—one question emerged as the central theme: *Who or what is shaping the financial habits and values of today's young people?* To answer this question, one has to think beyond the obvious and take inventory of all the influences that are competing for your child's time, attention, and money. As I detail in Part One, you might be surprised and disturbed by what you learn.

There are three reasons I was motivated to write this book. First is the reaction of parents who have attended the many workshops and events where I have spoken. Many of them encouraged me to write this book so the message could have an even wider audience.

Second, I hope this book will help parents gain confidence in their rightful roles as teachers and mentors in shaping their children's financial habits and values. In Part II, I have included many different ideas and suggestions to support those efforts.

My third reason is that knowledge is power. By sharing some of what I have learned from parents and their children during the last 14 years, it is my hope that more families will have a better sense of what they are up against. While understanding the technicalities of managing money is valuable, it is equally, if not more important, to know how companies relentlessly target children to buy their products. If parents don't understand how the latter is a barrier to learning the former, basic money management skills will become meaningless.

Much has changed since those early conversations with Sally back in Pennsylvania. What started as a little workshop in 1990 quickly grew on a regional and then a national level. By 1995, I had worked with hundreds of families. I kept hearing from parents that there was an enormous void in this field and that they were hungry for information that would support a values-based approach to teaching young people about money.

Soon after, Thrivent Financial (formerly known as Lutheran Brotherhood), the Fortune 500 financial services company where I worked, began receiving requests from media outlets across the country seeking more information about this approach.

Over the years, the core message has never wavered: Young people need caring and interested adults to help them develop healthy financial habits and values. And as you will see throughout the book, I think that is best accomplished by adopting a *share, save,* and *spend* philosophy.

I hope you will find the book's anecdotes helpful as you think about your own experiences and assess your own skills. In some instances, the names have been changed and the situation altered to protect the privacy of the people who shared their stories. In the end, I hope you will find comfort and encouragement in knowing you are not alone in your quest to teach financial balance.

Part ONE

Under the Spell of Hypnotic Consumption

Chapter ONE

Just Buy It!

When 20-year-old Melissa entered her sophomore year at the University of Missouri at Columbia, her parents felt confident that she was making good financial decisions. During the summer, Melissa had stayed in Missouri, rather than come home to suburban Minneapolis-St. Paul, just so she could qualify for in-state tuition, room and board, a savings of $9000 the first year. She also had worked full time as a waitress to build her savings.

That was September. Three months later, her parents' confidence in Melissa's money management skills was shattered. They discovered that Melissa had started using credit cards and now owed $2800.

During the summer, Melissa had grown accustomed to making and spending a lot of cash. At the start of the school year, she moved into a sorority where nice cars, nice clothes, and weekly visits to the tanning booth and nail salon were common. "She wanted it all," says her mother, Sue. "She wanted to look good, dress well. There's a lot of peer pressure, and she caved in."

Meanwhile, Melissa had cut back her work schedule to part-time hours. Her income didn't match her lifestyle, so she applied for a credit card from a booth on campus. "Everywhere she turned, somebody was offering her a credit card," Sue says. "Even the sorority had a program encouraging the girls to take out a sorority credit card."

Melissa bought into the lifestyle. She ate in higher-priced restaurants. She upgraded her wardrobe. More tanning. More nail jobs. More credit cards. Most cards had a limit of just $200 or $300. Even though her college fund covered all major expenses—tuition, room and board, books—by December she owed $2800 on 15 cards.

Sending your child off to college probably fills you with fear—of what your child might encounter and how he or she will handle the social, academic, and financial pressures. Have you, in 18 years of parenting, prepared your child for this leap toward independence? Will your child have the knowledge, values, and strength to make the right choices when you're not there to offer guidance? Will your child be able to manage money and avoid the financial troubles that developed so quickly for Melissa? Before you answer, consider three factors.

1. Melissa's $2800 in credit card debt is nearly average for college students. In 2001, the average undergraduate owed $2327 on plastic. According to student loan provider Nellie Mae, 21 percent have balances between $3000 and $7000.[1]

2. Melissa is not an "average" young adult. Like many first-borns, she is organized, responsible, reliable, and driven. She always worked hard to get good grades. Even as a young child, she showed solid money habits. She usually saved most of her allowance and was thoughtful on how she spent her money. To earn more spending money, she was a babysitter, then worked part time beginning at age

15. "She always seemed to have things under control," her mother says.

3. Melissa does not have "average" parents. Her father is president of the credit union for a Fortune 500 company. Her mother heads the financial services practice at a leading public relations agency. Both parents have expertise in personal finance and are experienced at talking about money issues. They helped their children develop their ability to manage money. Both parents are models of good money management. For example, Melissa watched her parents save $45,000 for her college fund.

"I would not have predicted that we would be in this situation," Sue says. That's just the point. If financial experts can't keep their child from tumbling into debt, if money problems can explode in the hands of a bright young woman like Melissa, what are the chances your child won't suffer a similar fate?

What's Going On?

More and more parents across the United States are troubled by their children's attitudes about money and spending. They see disturbing clues in the way children spend and in the way they pressure Mom and Dad to spend. It's not their imagination. A broad collection of government reports, university studies, and other research documents radical change in the relationship between kids and money. Across the board, trends suggest that young people are headed for trouble.

According to a national survey by the Center for a New American Dream, 87 percent of U.S. parents say that advertising and marketing aimed at children makes kids too materialistic. With this generation, what you wear, what you eat, and where you shop determine who you are. Brand conscious at ever younger ages and more intensely brand loyal with every year, American youth are willing to pay a premium for the right brands.[2]

This is not just kids preferring one flavor over another. To a young mind, brands are magical. They carry secret powers that make kids feel accepted. Young people walk around thinking, "I'm nothing without my Nike shoes, Tommy Hilfiger shirt, and can of Mountain Dew." Toss in peer pressure—the fact that people who matter are watching—and it's no wonder kids maintain a perpetual quest to have the latest, greatest whatever. This may explain the endless series of crises where buying the hot brand escalates to a matter of life or embarrassment.

Kids quickly learn that the pursuit of affluence is the American way. With ample nudging from advertisers, kids always have something new to add to their wish lists. Intent on making their kids happy, time-crunched parents eagerly grant their every wish. When a youngster's quality of life hinges on acceptance, and a new scooter or the latest jeans catches the attention of peers, kids soon see possessions as the route to happiness or, better yet, popularity.

Sound familiar? From toddlers to teens and even young adults, parents feel cause for alarm. Do your children know the value of a dollar? Do they save for the future? Do they make good financial decisions? Probably not. Messages about moderation and reality belong on the endangered list because the American consumer culture drowns out the voice of reason.

The old-time values of sacrifice, thrift, and satisfaction have been swept aside, replaced by a need for more and better possessions. Today, the norm is to aspire to luxuries, to believe that you deserve whatever you want, and to embrace debt to get what you want—and get it now. Of course, many parents themselves are caught up in this culture. While they spend more time in the pursuit of stuff, they have less time to guide their children toward a better way.

Many young people have expensive tastes, high expectations, and little sense of financial responsibility. Almost two-thirds of parents say that their own children define their self-worth in terms of possessions and that the problem has worsened over time. You've seen how kids seem to feel entitled to whatever they want whenever they want it. And, of course, price is no object, especially when Mom or Dad are paying. Chances are, your children often state what they should or deserve to have.[3]

Consider the cars many college students drive. If you've ever traversed a college parking lot, you will notice that many students drive better cars then the faculty or the president.

While their expectations are sky-high, most kids have never developed a down-to-earth sense of the value of money. As a 12- to 17-year-old, you may not have bothered to pick up a penny from the sidewalk, but the glint of silver probably caused a scramble. In a recent survey by Nuveen Investments, 58 percent of kids that age said they wouldn't bother to pick up anything less than a dollar.[4]

Neale Godfrey, chairman of the Children's Financial Network and author of books on money for parents and children, said she wasn't surprised because many high school students buy lunch—and throw away the change. When did coins become trash? Talk about short-sighted. Even if you believe that nothing worth buying costs less than $1, it doesn't take a Wall Street wizard to figure out that pocketing $.50 a day adds up to $2.50 a week or at least $10 a month.[5]

Children today live in a fantasy world that rejects traditional values and fails to prepare them for real-life money management as adults. To be young in the United States means living for the moment and reciting a new pledge of allegiance: "I want it all, and I want it now." An indulgent, upscale lifestyle serves as the modern standard. With their insatiable hunger for stuff, young people are passionate consumers.

They believe that money is meant to be spent. And they show little regard for the consequences of their financial decisions. From the preschooler who whines for another dollar, to the college student who graduates owing $10,000 on credit cards, U.S. children are the product of manipulation and temptation. Our consumer culture teaches kids to start spending and never stop. Marketing, peer pressure, TV, movies, and other voices of consumerism get inside kids' heads with their endless drone: "Buy this. Buy this. Buy this and this and this."

Day after day, year after year, these messages pound away at your child. The cumulative effect creates an overwhelming bias toward consumption over moderation. A generation that spends without thinking now resembles lemmings racing off a cliff. They have no clue that danger is near.

Undermining the hopes of parents, the consumer culture shapes your children in ways you may not like. It warps their perspective on what they need and seduces them into wanting more, more, and more. Big business is talking directly to your kids, trying to "pull their strings." Sophisticated marketing and advertising agencies understand how kids tick. Using child psychology and the latest insights on child behavior, they press kids' hot buttons to nudge them into action. In short, they target your child with manipulative tactics that border on mind control. Meanwhile, the rest of society—business, school, government, and religion—is doing little to protect kids from commercial forces or to prepare them to be rational consumers.

Stephen King couldn't have come up with a creepier scenario: Advertisers plant junior spies among our kids, enlist cartoon characters, pop stars, and professional athletes to gain their trust, exploit children's fear of being left out, disguise their messages as something other than advertising, and pay off school officials to let them get perversely close to children during the school day. The combined effect lures kids into spending with promises of nonstop fun and popularity.

"Hop on the merry-go-round and sing along with the happy music," says the chorus of advertisers. "And pay no attention to that feeling of spinning out of control." In this horror story, Mom and Dad come along for the ride. No one notices the ride spinning faster and faster. No one notices the long, sharp teeth and howling laughter of the advertisers. And no one shouts, "Stop! Let the children get off!"

What Lies Ahead?

High expectations and high-roller spending habits make a perilous combination. Today's youth burn through cash, often finding ways to blow every penny just in time for the next allowance or paycheck. Those spend-happy ways may seem innocent and harmless in an 8-year-old or 12-year-old. But that same youthful attitude at 16, 18, or 20 turns ominous.

For clues to what lies ahead for your child, take a look at today's 18- to 35-year-olds, a group that often lives paycheck to paycheck while trying to climb out of debt. Debt loads tend to be heaviest when people are young and starting their careers. This generation provides an extreme example of that rule.

"We're seeing students with $30,000 in student loans, $15,000 to pay off on credit cards, and they're going to earn $22,000 a year when they graduate," says Robert D. Manning, an economic sociologist and author of *Credit Card Nation: The Consequences of America's Addiction to Credit.* He foresees bankruptcy as a likely outcome for these recent graduates.[6]

"By almost every measure, young people are falling behind," *USA Today* recently reported. Consider the evidence:

- *Net worth.* While the median net worth of families rose for all other age groups between 1995 and 1998, the Federal

Reserve reports the net worth for the under-35 group declined from $12,700 to $9,000.[7]

- *Savings.* According to the U.S. Department of Commerce, savings as a percentage of after tax income has gone from a high of 9 percent in late 1992 to approximately 3.4 percent in 2002.[8]

- *Home equity.* Because young people tend to make smaller down payments and borrow against their equity, the average equity among homeowners younger than 35 dwindled from $57,100 in 1989 to about $49,200 in 1999, reports the Consumer Federation of America.[9]

- *Bankruptcy.* In 1997, the number of people filing for bankruptcy finally exceeded the number of people graduating from college. The fastest-growing segment of those filing for bankruptcy? People under 25. In 1991, about 60,000 young people filed for bankruptcy. By 2001, annual filings for the 25-and-under group jumped 150 percent to about 150,000.[10]

Financial Armageddon?

The United States, more than any other country, is at a critical financial crossroad. Our economy depends on voracious consumer appetites. In fact, consumer spending drives two-thirds of our nation's economic activity. Never was this more evident than after the terrorist attacks of September 11, 2001. Politicians pleaded with Americans to "do your part" by heading to the local shopping center. Urgent requests to hit the mall after such a horrific tragedy felt surreal, even for the neighborhood spendthrift. If anyone doubted the power of the individual consumer, doubt no more.

For the consumer culture to thrive, the next generation must be indoctrinated into the consumer lifestyle, which might be a house of cards. Herein lies the dilemma. The

10

country's economic success depends on Americans embracing the consumer lifestyle, but the consumer lifestyle is hazardous to a young person's financial and emotional health. Although we haven't been asked to make a conscious choice between the economy and the welfare of children, society appears content in allowing business to continue hypnotizing young people to spend early and spend often.

As a result, the country now faces a crisis because children are growing up without balanced financial values or a well-thought approach to how they use money—I call it a financial philosophy. Today, every young person is at risk of growing up with underdeveloped values and overdeveloped expectations. The consumer culture works overtime to convince young Americans they deserve a fantasy lifestyle. It jams the signal when you try to teach your own children and replaces your outlook with a distorted view. When it comes to spending, kids are confused on what is and isn't important. They struggle to differentiate between the things they need and those they want. Lacking priorities, they have trouble saying no to anything that looks tempting.

Young people look for direction on a variety of life issues. They get plenty of guidance on sex, drugs, alcohol, tobacco, careers, dating, and so on. Unfortunately, on money, they often get silence. Parents tend to be overwhelmed with the subject of money. Few parents have formal training in finance. Even fewer have formulated their own financial values and financial philosophy. Most of us are caught up in the consumer society, so kids rarely see role models for moderation. Consequently, young people don't know how to manage money.

Beware of a financial Armageddon, in which young adults crash and burn in overwhelming debt and bankruptcy. As with everything about growing up, the stakes get higher with age. The nickels, dimes, and quarters spent on candy and trinkets escalate to hundreds and thousands of dollars on cars, motorcycles, stereos, spring break trips, and more. What will happen when your children become young adults? When Mom and Dad aren't there with a voice of caution? When those high expectations collide with limited income?

Like Melissa, the college student who was lured into trouble with credit cards, most young adults cover up their debt out of fear, guilt, and shame. Parents rarely know the extent of their child's debt until it becomes overwhelming. Once Melissa's spree was discovered, her father arranged a consolidation loan to pay off the credit cards. For two years, she'll pay $113 a month—a big chunk of her $200 to $300 monthly income during the school year.

"The good news is that we caught it as early as we did," says her mother, Sue. "My biggest concern is that she may not have learned from this. I don't think she would hesitate to do it again." Two months after her parents stepped in, Melissa bought a one-week trip to Cancun, Mexico, for spring break because she felt she deserved a getaway. When Melissa asked her mom for a loan so she could have spending money, Sue declined. "I do worry that she could get farther into debt before she gets out of debt," Sue says. "She hasn't hit bottom yet."

Young Americans teeter on a financial tightrope, and they have lousy balance. In the words of *USA Today*, "Like no other generation, today's 18- to 35-year-olds have grown up with a culture of debt—a product of easy credit, a booming economy and expensive lifestyles."[11] Assuming full employment would last forever, they spent freely during the economic bonanza of the 1990s. The fall of Internet companies and the softening of the economy beginning in 2000 came as a shock to many under 30. Now that they're accustomed to living in debt, how many are just a layoff away from bankruptcy?

A Financial Intervention

We, as a nation, are caught up in hypnotic consumption with spending so ingrained it has become a reflex for most young people. See something you want, and your hand instinctively reaches for money. The consumer culture makes it acceptable to have no financial discipline. Our culture speaks loud and clear: "Forget about saving. If you want it, buy it. If you can't afford it, charge it. Don't worry about the cost. Don't worry about how much you already owe. Life is fun and exciting when you go anywhere and do anything you like."

We laugh and joke about shopaholics, credit fiends who can fan out their cards like a bridge hand, and others who don't know when to stop spending. Most of us, aware of the consequences, know better than to let a friend drive drunk. So why do we let people, including our own children, adopt self-destructive spending habits?

This book is a financial "intervention." Solving any problem begins with awareness. I want to wake this country from its trance. In particular, I hope parents see the consumer culture for what it really is: legalized corruption of children. Parents simply haven't been alert to the changing environment, so, instead of striving to counter those influences, they unwittingly play along.

The first half of this book outlines the disturbing facts about the country's possession-crazed youth and the society that has distorted their values. The second half carries a message of hope: You can help your child break free from materialism. It also serves as a guide to shaping appropriate financial habits and balanced financial values—the strong foundation that prepares kids to be intelligent consumers.

I didn't realize how far the effect of consumerism on children had advanced until 1990, when a religious educator at a church in Pennsylvania asked me for help. She had a sense that children in the church had fallen out of balance on money issues. The kids seemed swept up in spending for all kinds of objects and showed no sign that sharing had a place in their lives. Then, as a financial adviser, I developed financial education workshops for young people and their parents. My early experiences with kids were enlightening. When I asked them to list all the things they could do with their money, they never thought of sharing. There we were in a church on a Sunday morning, but it didn't dawn on them that sharing was an option. I was dumbfounded.

Today, "Parents, Kids & Money" and "Parents, Teens & Money" have evolved into interactive workshops for tweens (8- to 12-year-olds), teens (13- to 18-year-olds), and their parents. In giving these workshops, I've had a chance to talk with thousands of kids and their parents.

It is abundantly clear that parents fear for their children and don't know how to help. They see the methodical assault of advertising. They see in their children an incessant need to *have*—to the point where their self-esteem hinges on the brand of their possessions. They wonder and dread where the momentum is taking the kids.

They don't like what is happening to their children, but they feel powerless and overwhelmed. They don't know how to talk to their kids about money—a topic that in many ways is just as intimidating and sensitive as sex. Many doubt their own ability to explain financial issues. And, considering parents spend an average of 40 minutes a week with their kids, most can't find time to discuss their concerns about money.[12]

More than anything else, this book emphasizes why parents need to talk about money with their kids. The fact that government, schools, business, and faith-based organizations have abdicated their role in preparing or protecting our children means that parents are on their own. It's you against society, corporate America, and all forms of media. There has never been a more urgent need for parents to take an active role in setting financial boundaries and priorities.

You are your child's best hope for growing up resistant to the consumer culture. Parents have great influence in shaping their kids' values, priorities, and habits. And the sooner you realize that virtually every message your child hears about money promotes spending, the more prepared you will be to counter with messages on the value of saving and the joy of sharing. It's up to you to teach your child about financial balance. If you don't, you entrust your child's values formation to the marketplace. Countless other voices will tell your child what he or she needs. And make no mistake, your child will listen!

Money Talks

Many of the chapters in the book conclude with a series of questions called "Money Talks." They are designed to build on the themes from the chapter and can be used as a springboard for additional conversations and reflection.

- Have you or your child ever covered up a purchase? Why?
- In what ways are you a model of healthy money management?
- What concerns you about your child's attitudes about money and possessions?
- Would your child pick up a quarter or throw away a quarter?

- What makes you think your child does or doesn't understand the consequences of his or her financial decisions?
- Who were your financial role models? What did they teach you?
- Have you ever had money problems? If so, what did it take to recover?
- Why is it important for your child to learn to manage money?

Chapter TWO

The Gotta-Have-It-Now Generation

A s her two daughters grew older and more skilled in the art of persuasion, Celia realized that back-to-school shopping grew more painful. When Celia's oldest daughter, Amber, now 14, walked through the doors of the mall, all rational behavior vanished.

The battle lines were drawn on the parent list of needs and the Amber list of wants. Amber wanted the designer jeans at $90 a pop and Mom wanted "Brand X" for $40. There was pouting, there was stomping, there was whining at a pitch that made other shoppers turn to catch a glimpse of the show. Amber used every imaginable tactic to convince Mom that "I will be so happy if you just buy me the jeans I want." And so it went with the shoes, the shirts, and the makeup. For Celia, a poster in the window of a clothing store for teen girls cast the final blow: "I want it. I need it. I have to have it."

Is there a parent in this country who hasn't heard those words? Amber is part of an entire generation that lives by a simple motto: "I gotta have it now." Translation: I need whatever I want, whenever I want it. American kids expect nothing less, and they usually get it.

If you feel that no home could be as bad as your own during back-to-school shopping, think again. School shopping, second only to the holiday season in boosting retail sales, costs U.S. households an average of nearly $500 per child.[1] Why has this become such an expensive and painful ordeal? It is because kids are demanding. They know what they gotta have, and they don't care what it costs you.

"This generation is the 'I want' generation," says author and clinical psychologist Mary Pipher. "They have been educated to entitlement and programmed for discontent. Ads have encouraged this generation to have material expectations they can't fulfill."[2]

With the Gotta-Have-It-Now generation, there's always something else they can't live without. In the '90s, the roster of essentials included limited-edition Beanie Babies stuffed animals; Sony, Sega, and Nintendo game consoles; assorted video games; and Pokémon collectible game pieces. It's never about being satisfied; it's about getting and wanting more. And no child is immune.

Spending Habits

Call them crazes or manias, these mass demands for objects—just like the battles over school shopping—are irrational and irritating for parents. You could dismiss these requests as an innocent phase of adolescence, but join me in a more thoughtful look at this behavior. Upon closer review, you'll see a disturbing problem brewing just under the surface of the incessant consumer demands of young Americans. The "high" young people experience when their wants are finally met may be the beginning of a lifetime struggle with financial habits and boundaries. Could the combination of young people's appetite for possessions and parents' desire to keep their children content give rise to disturbing new behaviors? Is materialism a new form of dependency? Are young people somehow growing up addicted to spending?

Addiction

Any compulsive, habitual behavior that limits the freedom of human desire. It is caused by the attachment, or nailing, of desire to specific objects.[3] We live in a society gripped by all kinds of addictions—gambling, alcohol, drugs, sex, food, TV, and the Internet. The financial attitudes and behavior of many children now bear an eerie parallel to addiction. Their time, energy, and money are getting sucked deeper and deeper into a way of life that makes them numb to the ultimate consequences of indulgent spending. Consider some of the following classic symptoms of addiction behavior. Then compare them to the attitudes and behavior manifested in young people today.

Tolerance

The phenomenon of always wanting or needing more of the addictive behavior or the object of attachment in order to feel satisfied.[4] What used to be adequate doesn't cut it anymore. Many parents talk about their kids becoming bored with what they have. By the time his daughters reached age 10 and 12, Jon noticed that his girls lost interest in going to McDonald's. When the family went out for dinner, the girls wanted to go to a restaurant with table service. They wanted appetizers. They wanted additional side orders. They wanted dessert. And the folks cringed when the waitress handed them the bill. The family vacation often upgrades over time, in part because the kids want a more exciting destination.

Then comes the need to travel with their peers. Jebah, a college junior, described how several of her friends *had* to go somewhere exotic for spring break, even though they didn't have the cash—more than $1000 apiece. "No big deal, let's just charge it," she rationalized. "After all, what are these credit cards for? Having fun today!"

Self-Deception

A person's thinking becomes increasingly twisted until fantasy becomes reality and he or she lives more and more in a world where there are no consequences for bad decisions.[5] For many young people, the fantasy lies in what's affordable. There's nothing wrong with window shopping. Everybody wishes they had something that's beyond their reach. The problem is in ignoring limitations. A lot of kids have mastered the art of ignoring financial limits, while a lot of parents have mastered the art of giving in. Michael grew up convincing his workaholic, credit-card-dependent parents that buying him stuff was the secret to his happiness. By never learning how to live within his means, Michael at age 34 struggles to keep ahead of bill collectors. As with many other addictions, Michael's parents unknowingly passed their self-destructive behavior on to their son. When it comes to the kids, too often money's no object. Meanwhile, instead of accepting responsibility, many teens become adept at dodging consequences. While in high school, Abby got her own membership at a video store and rented a stack of movies. She returned the movies a couple weeks later. Rather than pay a fine approaching $100, she never went back to that store.

Loss of Willpower

The mind asserts that it in fact can control the behavior. At certain points, it even encourages making resolutions to stop. It

20

knows such resolutions are likely to fail, and when they do, the addictive behavior will have a stronger foothold than ever.[6] How many kids have the strength to say no to temptation? Chrissy adores black platform shoes and now has more than a dozen pairs. Liz, 16, eventually closed her new checking account because she kept bouncing checks. She could see how little money was in her account, but buying that new sweater at the moment was more important than the $26 overdraft penalty the bank would charge her later. For many young people, this loss of control starts small, then escalates. More than 63 percent of college students in the United States know someone who dropped out or reduced their class load so they could earn more money to resolve financial problems.[7] Tom is like a lot of college students. He owes $3000 to Visa and manages his debt by applying for additional credit cards.

Distortion of Attention

Our minds are often able to keep these addictions hidden, even from ourselves, as long as we are getting a sufficient supply of the object of attachment and are experiencing no great conflict about it.[8] The prevailing attitude suggests that it's not who you are inside that counts, it's what you own. Advertising, which plays on insecurities, is a major contributor to this distortion by planting this idea in kids' heads: "If I just buy this, I'll be happy." When she feels bad or things just aren't going her way, Jessica buys something. It may be clothes. It may be food, but she has to buy. And then she feels better . . . for a while. Until it happens again, and she buys once more. In the addiction cycle, an urge builds, then the act of drinking or gambling or buying is followed by the high. Then comes withdrawal, followed by pain, which can be mental, emotional, physical, or spiritual, and the process starts over.

Growing Preoccupation

The person begins to anticipate the addictive process during daytime activities and shows a growing interest in actions that are both unneeded and unnecessary.[9] Millions of children were introduced to this symptom in the wild and crazy fantasy world of Pokémon. One father described the rabid nature of his young son and how he would insist on making daily trips to the drugstore to buy more cards: "I would pick him up from school and he would 'instruct' me to swing by the store. He would tell stories about how he and his friends had talked about the cards all day at school." How many teens visit tanning salons weekly or more often—in the middle of summer? How many teens spend their free time in a shopping mall? At the height of the Beanie Babies craze, Jennifer had over 75 Beanie Babies in her bedroom. As an 8-year-old, she constantly bugged Mom or Dad to drive her around town to snap up the latest offering. When Mom and Dad didn't comply, she unleashed a temper tantrum, complete with feet stomping, door slamming, and screaming.

Growing Rigidity in Lifestyle

Self-imposed rules begin to change what the person can and cannot do.[10] Just look at what kids choose or refuse to wear. Brand names or bust! There is a reason that Abercrombie, Nike, and the Gap, to name a few, spend millions for mind and market share. If they get you early enough, they've got you for good. Martha has three high-school-age sons who buy their clothes only at Abercrombie & Fitch. Barb confesses that her younger daughter gets all her undergarments at Victoria's Secret. In contrast, try to find a teen who will lace up a no-name brand of tennis shoes. Connie's 14-year-old daughter laughed when she suggested looking for clothes at Sears. When your concern over a price tag conflicts with your child's commitment to fashion, watch out. Your rational thought likely triggers an irrational retort. If you press the issue, you're in for a battle.

Financial Difficulties

Addictive behavior may create additional expenses, reduce income by interfering with work, and impair ability to make rational decisions that involve money.[11] Until they're old enough to work, your children's spending habits create financial difficulties only for you. In time, they might blow money on late fees, overdraft penalties, and additional charges on a cell phone, but managing money rarely becomes a problem for your kids until they get a credit card. Then they can suddenly spend more money than they have and make the leap into debt. If take-home pay is not sufficient to cover the expenses, bills pile up and remain unpaid. Credit cards get maxed out. Ryan, 22, described the day he gave in to the $7000 debt he had amassed: "I was staring at my credit card statement, in a trance. Looking around at all the crap I had purchased, I finally decided to accept that I was going to be in debt for the rest of my life. I was overcome with anxiety and fear, but somehow I managed to convince myself that it was going to be okay."

Materialism is a stealthy addiction. There are no warning labels, no awareness campaigns, and no catchy slogans to caution young people against greed or debt or bankruptcy. For some, as with other addictions, the hook is immediate. Whether the first purchase for a young child or the swipe of a credit card for a college freshman, the result can be the same. The high exhilarates, and the need for more grows with each purchase. For others, it progresses gradually—a missed payment here, a second mortgage for consumer debts there. Regardless, once materialism owns you, breaking free can be long and arduous.

Young people today are incredibly susceptible to the siren song of hypnotic consumption. In their brief lifetimes, they have been lulled into complacency about financial responsibility while living in a warp-speed world that blurs appropriate financial boundaries. There are four factors that make kids more vulnerable than ever to addictive materialism.

1. Confusion between needs and wants. If you ever need to quiet a room of young people, ask them to describe the difference between a need and a want. Guaranteed silence. I frequently speak to groups of young people all over the country and nothing perplexes them more than this question. It's as if they have no internal compass to guide their decisions.

   When the same question is put to my 94-year-old grandmother, she handles it with ease. The difference is startling! One generation grew up working for and appreciating everything they have. Another generation grows up with everything handed to them on a silver platter and screams for more. Some people mistakenly refer to this as progress.

   Confusion has steadily built over the last 30 years. As the pace of people's lives has increased, juggling of countless tasks has become more complicated. Few parents find time to teach their kids about money. Meanwhile, advertisers have dedicated a growing volume of resources to convincing young people that they need whatever the company sells.

2. Peer pressure. Out of all issues that kids struggle with, peer pressure ranks number one with girls and number three with boys, according to a California State University study.[12] It starts early—little stuff like video games and toys, but quickly moves to clothing, friends, and appear-

ance. God help the young person who falls on the wrong side of peer pressure. The epicenter of this emotional earthquake can be pinpointed to looking right, acting right, talking right, and living right.

Kris remembers the relentless harassing she endured as a 16-year-old sophomore upon moving from a small town in Wisconsin to a suburb of Minneapolis: "Our family didn't have much money, and my clothes were mostly generic brands. It was tough enough trying to fit in as the 'new kid.' But I had to overcome how I looked as well. As much as I liked school, I dreaded the thought of facing another day feeling horrible." Kids across the United States share similar experiences. The pressure to look like you have money even when you don't goes beyond any rational measure. That's one major reason why Philadelphia Public Schools and other school districts have adopted mandatory school uniforms.

3. Poor financial literacy. At a time when the adult world fixates on the daily movement of the stock markets, financial literacy for young people is bad and getting worse. In a 1997 survey, high school seniors answered correctly an average of 57 percent of questions on income, money management, saving and investing, and spending and credit. As a whole, they failed in financial literacy. In 2002, scores fell to an average of 50 percent.[13] That's certainly not a confidence booster if you are Federal Reserve Chairman Alan Greenspan and concerned about the future of our economy.

4. Warped perspective. With advertisers telling kids what they truly need, peer pressure dictating what's acceptable, and financial illiteracy clouding reality, kids tend to get skewed in their thinking. You know that things are distorted when your child rationalizes a purchase by saying, "Everyone else is buying it, so why shouldn't I?" At some

point, your child has tuned out the cost, your budget, and other prudent factors. Ultimately, kids don't know what they don't know. They struggle because they don't have the tools to question their own decisions. If the compass spins around, giving no clue to true north, how can we expect children to find their way?

If young people are becoming addicted to spending, what does that say about their parents? Are parents actually enablers, the people who allow an addiction to develop and persist? If so, then caving in to a child's request for a toy or a treat could be seen as part of a contributing pattern. A vow to give your child everything you never had suddenly starts to look like a misguided show of love.

Grace, a 52-year-old mother of a college senior, said she and her husband tried to protect their son from poor financial decisions as a child. "He never seemed to have any money even though we were always handing it out. Periodically, we'd get concerned and have him write down how he spent his money, but we never followed through," she said.

Rather than correcting the small transgressions at an early age, the problem festered and grew. Now their son worries about finding an apartment after college because his credit rating is so bad. Grace admits it was always easier to give him what he wanted, and she worries he will face a lifetime of financial difficulty. In the future, Grace and her husband must decide when to practice tough love as they face the recurring temptation to bail out their son.

Ultimately, parents need to decide what habits and values you pass on to your kids. Do your actions teach a balanced approach to money management? Or do they instill unhealthy patterns of consumer addiction?

Money Talks

- What makes you think your child is a member of the Gotta-Have-It-Now generation?
- If you disagree with your child about a purchase, what makes it escalate to an argument?
- If you have gone to an extreme to make your child happy during a consumer craze, how did that feel? Was it important for your child? In hindsight, how do you feel about your actions?
- What financial habits do you and your child share? In which do you differ?
- Consider each of the addictive symptoms—tolerance, self-deception, loss of willpower, distortion of attention, growing preoccupation, growing rigidity in lifestyle, and financial difficulties. Do you see signs in your child? In yourself? In your parents?
- How does peer pressure influence your child's purchasing decisions? How does it influence your purchasing decisions?
- What makes you think your child has a warped perspective on money management?
- What actions have you taken that could be seen as enabling addiction behavior in your child?

Chapter THREE

A Branded New World

It's a far different world from when you were growing up. Let's look back 25 or 30 years, when you were about their age, to recall the environment at that time and the options that were available to you. Then we'll fast forward to today. You'll see a dramatic change, with a major shift toward upscale choices, greater convenience, and other aspects of a free-spending lifestyle.

Just in electronics, compare the home in which you grew up to your home today. The average American child lives in a household with three televisions, two VCRs, three radios, three tape players, two CD players, a video game system, and a computer (see Tables 3.1 and 3.2). Look inside their bedrooms and you'll find that 53 percent of kids—including more than one-fourth of those age two to four—have their own television.[1]

Table 3.1 Proportion of Time Each Medium Contributes to Total Media Budget by Age

Medium	Age 2 to 18	Age 2 to 7	Age 8 to 13	Age 14 to 18
Television	42%	46%	44%	36%
Other non-interactive screen	13%	12%	15%	11%
Video games	5%	3%	7%	4%
Print media	12%	18%	10%	8%
Audio media	22%	17%	17%	34%
Computer	5%	3%	7%	7%

Source: Kids & Media @ The New Millennium, Kaiser Family Foundation, 1999.

Think about what was true for you as a child and what your child expects today. Face it, your child is from a different planet. Home may still be called Earth, but it bears little resemblance to the place where you grew up. Because their environment is so different, today's kids can't help but think and act differently.

Table 3.2 Media Availability in Children's Homes: Children 2–18 (Percent of Children Who Live in Homes)

Medium	Average	With 1+	2+	3+
TV	2.9	99	88	60
VCR	1.8	97	58	21
Radio	3.1	97	85	63
Tape player	2.6	94	71	47
CD player	2.1	90	59	35
Video game player	1.4	70	38	18
Computer	1.0	69	21	6
Cable/satellite TV		74		
Premium cable channels		44		
Internet access		45		
CD-ROM		59		

Source: Kids & Media @ The New Millennium, Kaiser Family Foundation, 1999.

Trillion-Dollar Babies

American children, from newborns through age 22, spend and influence the spending of nearly $1 trillion per year. Dr. James McNeal, kid marketing expert, estimates that tweens (ages 8 to 12) and teens (ages 13 to 17) directly or indirectly influence household spending of $450 to $500 billion annually.[2] *American Demographics* magazine claims that tweens and teens spend over $150 billion of their own money each year.[3] When you toss in those younger than age 8 and older than 17 plus all the influence these young people have on grandparent purchases, this group is easily a $1 trillion per year market.

Marketing experts track three kinds of youth spending:

1. Direct spending of their own money grows as kids get older, get jobs, and gain independence.
2. Direct influence on parent spending includes kids' hints, requests, and demands for things for themselves plus their input on family decisions.[4]
3. Indirect influence includes parent spending on children's needs and their known preferences.[5]

Including college-age adults, who often have some financial dependence on their parents, this lucrative market of young people totals close to 80 million or nearly one-third of the U.S. population.[6] Most are echo boomers or Generation Y—the offspring of the baby boom generation and the largest population group since their parents. In fact, teenagers are the nation's fastest-growing population group. By 2010, says market researcher Teenage Research Unlimited, teens will number 33.9 million, the largest teen market ever.[7]

According to Ken Gronbach, generational marketer and president of KGA Communications, kids under age 20 spend five times more—in inflation-adjusted dollars—than their parents did at the same age.[8] Youth spending continues to grow at an accelerating pace. Dr. James McNeal, author of *The Kids Market: Myths and Realities*, found that spending by children age 4 to 12 roughly doubled during each decade in the 1960s, 1970s and 1980s. In the 1990s, it tripled. And, in contrast to the 1960s, when children spent money mainly on confections, McNeal says, two-thirds of their money today goes for toys, apparel, entertainment, and health and beauty.[9] "These are young kids who have more disposable income than any other generation before them," says Sarah Scheuer, a spokeswoman for the National Retail Federation.[10]

At the same time, parents give their kids heftier allowances than they received at the same age, and teens work more hours at a younger age than their parents did. Meanwhile, a more participatory parenting style combined with lower resistance among overloaded parents in dual-income families and single-parent families give kids more clout than ever in family buying decisions. While children's income grew 15 to 20 percent per year during the latter half of the 1990s, their influence on parent spending rose at an even faster rate.[11]

Some changes in youth spending and influence reflect advances in technology. For the most part, though, this new world was created by an increasingly aggressive and sophisticated marketplace. Corporate America, salivating over the huge amount of money spent on and by children, has been working overtime to give American kids countless reasons and ways to spend their money and their parents'.

Viewed separately, the products highlighted in this chapter seem innovative. Viewed as a whole, they illustrate corporate strategies to capture and stimulate youth spending by molding the modern lifestyle. These forces become apparent when we compare your youth to your child's world in several major categories.

Toys

Then. Toys were basic. There were board games (Monopoly and Life), other games (Yahtzee and Racko!), active toys (yo-yos and jump ropes), building sets (Tinker Toys and Lincoln Logs), and toys for imaginative role-playing (Barbie and GI Joe). Except for a bike, Lionel train or slot-car race-track, few items in the toy department back then topped $20. Your toys got a lot of use until they broke or you out-grew them. And your entire collection of toys fit on the shelves and closet in your bedroom.

Now. Toys have gone upscale and abundant. You proba-bly never owned a squirt gun that cost more than $1 or shot more than 10 feet. But the Super Soaker, which industry ex-perts call the world's most powerful and popular squirt gun, is in a class by itself. Its 14 models cost up to $60 and fire volleys of high-pressure water up to 50 feet.[12] Meanwhile, many fam-ilies have designated a playroom for their kids, in part because the kids' toys are too plentiful to fit in the bedroom closet. Fa-vorite toys have a short life expectancy because every day brings the possibility of something new and more exciting.

Barbie is one of the few toys from your generation that remains a hit with kids today. Otherwise, electronics have conquered the toy department. From 2000 to 2001, video game sales rocketed 43 percent to $9.4 billion.[13] You can still buy Monopoly and Yahtzee, but now they're also available as computer software or as a hand-held electronic game. Sales of sophisticated electronic toys incorporating the latest chip technology, like the popular robotic puppies, ap-proached $1 billion in 2000, nearly double the previous year.[14] See Table 3.3 for wholesale toy sales breakdown.

Think back to when you were eight years old. What would your response have been if asked to name your fa-vorite gift? After you have given this some thought, review

Table 3.3 Wholesale Toy Sales ($ in millions)

Category	2001	2000	Change
Video games	$9409	$6581	+43%
Action figures and accessories	$1618	$1187	+36%
Building and construction	$882	$722	+22%
Ride-ons	$773	$664	+17%
Infant and preschool	$3154	$2772	+14%
Arts and crafts	$2630	$2357	+12%
Dolls and accessories	$3061	$2835	+8%
Vehicles	$2821	$2624	+8%
Models and accessories	$281	$266	+6%
All other toys	$2703	$2681	+1%
Learning and exploration	$464	$491	−6%
Games and puzzles	$2237	$2492	−10%
Plush	$2031	$2336	−13%
Pretend play	$479	$565	−15%
Trading cards and accessories	$318	$440	−28%
Sports	$1528	$2135	−29%

Source: The NPD Group and Toy Industry Association.

the following list and consider how the answers have changed (especially in dollar value) in the past 30 years.

FAVORITE GIFTS FOR KIDS AGE 8 TO 12

- Big screen television for my room
- Hawaiian cruise
- My own cell phone
- iBook laptop computer
- Family trip to Disney World
- Coke machine for my room
- Swimming pool

Source: The Zandl Group.

The Modern Razor Blade

Now claiming 27 percent of the toy market, video games stand as the most dominant player in the toy aisle. So much has happened since 1975, when Sears inked a one-year deal with Atari to be the exclusive distributor of Pong, the pioneering video game.[15]

Much like the early marketing ploy of giving away razors to stimulate the sale of razor blades, the manufacturers sell Sony PlayStation 2, Microsoft Xbox, and Nintendo GameCube game consoles at a loss to create demand for video games. Games sell at a high margin, producing royalties galore for the system manufacturers. Of course, the fun is in the games, and having the system provides an ongoing reason to buy more games. In 2001, NPD FunWorld reports, 141.5 million video games sold for $4.6 billion.[16]

Kids under 14 make up 20 to 25 percent of the market and are the fastest growing segment. Marketers who secure product placement in video games get the advantage of repetition. When a snowboard manufacturer places its gear in Sony's "Cool Boarders" games, kids see the products 100 times or more before they tire of playing it. Now you can understand why so many companies are desperately seeking exposure in the latest video game.[17]

Playing on Friendship

If your kids own a Barbie car, a Tickle Me Elmo doll, a Mickey Mouse wristwatch or a Batman Halloween costume, you understand the appeal of licensed products. About 40 percent of all toys carry some sort of license, meaning a manufacturer pays a licensing fee for the right to produce a product bearing a popular character's name or image.[18] More often than not, licensing appears on a product that a child might not want or notice without the connection to these imaginary friends. In short, licensing exploits a child's attachment to fictional characters.

Now a standard method of selling to children, licensing exploded in popularity among manufacturers after the May 1977 opening of the film *Star Wars*. The original trilogy racked up $4.5 billion in sales of action figures and all sorts of other licensed merchandise.[19]

As a result, virtually every movie, television show, and product that appeals to children can be found on licensed products. The Sesame Workshop, producer of Sesame Street and other popular kids' shows, is a significant player in the toy market. With more than 400 licenses, thousands of products are produced in partnership with firms like Mattel, Sony, Kmart, Keebler, and Procter & Gamble. In 1996 and 1997, Sesame Workshop had the leading toys in the United States: Tickle Me Elmo and Sing and Snore Ernie. In 2000, Sesame Workshop generated over $132 million in publishing, program, and product licensing royalties.[20]

One Is Not Enough

Barbie, who turned 40 in 1999, was a pioneer at pitching the notion that one outfit just won't do. A billion-dollar business for Mattel, the Barbie line includes a multitude of swimsuits, evening gowns, and shoes that encourage girls to build a wardrobe for the fashion doll.[21]

Likewise, the Pokémon game encouraged kids to become more competitive players by collecting more game pieces. Beanie Babies, the biggest selling toy of the 1990s, used a limited-edition approach that injected a sense of urgency into buying the stuffed animals whenever they were available. With the focus on collecting assorted animals, most kids and many parents lost track of how much they were spending on critters that merely take up space. Priced at $5, Beanie Babies matched what many kids received in weekly allowance.

Food

Then. Aside from sugared cereals, kids ate the same food as grown-ups. Families only occasionally visited restaurants, although teens enjoyed a limited choice of fast-food restaurants.

Now. Active kids eat on the run. Busy schedules make family dinners a fading tradition. When time permits, meals are quick and easy. Otherwise, grab something for the car or pick up something along the way. Whatever you want is always nearby.

Food Is Everywhere

No matter where your kids go, they'll find something to eat. Convenience stores and gas stations that double as grocery stores offer snacks and a growing menu of foods on every busy street. Where there's one fast-food restaurant, you're just as likely to find five or six more. As of November 2002, McDonald's had nearly 29,000 worldwide locations, and Subway, Burger King, KFC, and Pizza Hut each had more than 11,000.[22] Shopping centers tempt teens and others with the crowd-pleasing variety of food courts. Kiosks sell cookies, pretzels, and other specialties in airports, shopping centers, and other places with a steady flow of foot traffic. After hours and in out-of-the-way locations, vending machines spit out an expanding selection of candy, salty snacks, soft drinks, sports drinks, and juices. The message is clear: If you're hungry, buy something now.

Convenience Is King

When your kids get hungry, they have countless options for foods that are ready to eat or can be heated quickly. Want a fresh bag of popcorn? Three minutes in the microwave, and it's yours with no mess. Convenience foods of all kinds are far more likely to be found in homes where teens reside. Nearly 90 percent of kids prepare something to eat for them-selves.[23] Of course, preparation usually means zapping a bowl in the microwave or popping a frozen pastry in the toaster.

Kids go for mobile foods, too. Yoplait Go-Gurt, yogurt in a squeeze tube, and juice boxes incorporate packaging in-novations that make it easy to carry foods that usually re-quire a spoon or refrigeration. McDonald's Egg McMuffin made a breakfast of Canadian bacon and eggs a hand-held meal by loading them on an English muffin. Hot Pockets, sold frozen, make a gooey sandwich manageable by encasing the contents in a hand-held crust. Hey, kids, whatever you want will be ready in a flash and handy to take along.

Dining Out As a Way of Life

No longer a luxury or a quick alternative, restaurants have become ingrained in the American family's busy schedule. The share of food dollars spent away from home climbed to an all-time high of 47 percent of food expenditures in 1998, says the U.S. Census Bureau. The National Restaurant Asso-ciation predicts that Americans will spend more than $400 billion dining out in 2002 and within the next few years will spend half of their food budgets away from home.[24]

"We've really shifted from being a leisure sector to be-ing an essential part of people's lives," says Steven Anderson, President and CEO of the National Restaurant Association.

Among teens, fast food rules. In a Public Health Institute survey of 12- to 17-year-olds, one-third said they eat at least one meal or snack from a fast-food restaurant on any given day.[25]

Restaurants Compete for Kids' Meals

Knowing that kids bring Mom and Dad, a broad range of restaurants try to be the name kids call out when they say, "Let's go to. . . ."

The competition is fiercest among fast-food restaurants, where McDonald's reigns as the acknowledged master of marketing to kids. McDonald's is the favorite brand of fast food among kids age seven and under, James McNeal says, because the company understands that kids want to play. From playgrounds to Happy Meals containing a free toy to licensing promotions with Disney and others, McDonald's works hard to influence kids on their restaurant choice.[26]

With licensing deals, fast-food chains double their kid appeal. The chance to get a special toy related to their heroes boosts the odds that kids will ask to go there soon. McDonald's and Burger King made it standard industry practice to cross-sell kids' meals with licensed merchandise, often related to a recent movie. Cross promoting is everywhere, and just about every company will align with another company if it helps move their product.

In early 2002, Burger King joined forces with X-Men, the superheroes featured in comic books and a feature film. Every premium kids' meal included one of eight 3-inch mini–CD-ROMs, one of eight collectible figures, and a fancy display stand. Talk about drawing power. Kids love superheroes. The collectible angle makes kids want to visit the restaurant eight times to get the complete set. The CD is a digital comic book—a computer game with content created specifically for Burger King by Marvel Interactive. And the CD is a 3-inch size versus the standard 5-inch size.[27]

"Kids love 'mini' versions of products," a Burger King spokesperson said at the time, adding that the company included the CD-ROM "because computer penetration finally supports a mass-audience promotion."[28]

Designed Especially for Kids

Products developed and marketed for children populate nearly every aisle of every supermarket. Start with the cereal aisle, where Tony the Tiger, the Trix Rabbit, Toucan Sam, the Cheerios Honey Bee, Cap'n Crunch, and other cartoon spokesmen pitch sugared cereals.

Licensing has transformed ordinary products into kiddie food. *Blue's Clues* appears on Kraft Macaroni & Cheese and Mott's berry-flavored applesauce. Sesame Street characters appear on Keebler snack crackers and cookies. Rugrats appear on Mott's fruit-punch-flavored applesauce and Popsicles.

Oscar Mayer Lunchables, originally a clever way for Kraft to combine its crackers, meats, and cheese in one package, soon morphed into a kid's meal that can include a Capri Sun juice drink and a treat, such as M&M's, Butterfinger, or Snickers. For many youngsters, Lunchables replace the brown-bag lunch at school, daycare, and day camp.

Children sparked the explosion of packaged juices and drinks. They also inspired new shapes, colors, flavors, packaging, and other features. The yogurt section now features brightly colored kid-oriented flavors. Kemp's includes little vanilla-cookie spoons with its yogurt cartons for kids. Popsicle makes crayon-shaped juice bars. Cookies, crackers, and frozen waffles come in mini sizes that kids see as

39

more fun and few parents realize are more expensive. In one of the latest trends, a Dannon yogurt drink and Nestlé flavored milk feature plastic bottles that are easier for kids to grip.

Introducing the Unhealthy, High-Fat American Diet

About half of all advertising aimed at kids pitches food. And four out of five food ads sell sugary cereal, soft drinks, fast food or salty snacks, says Margo Wootan, director of nutrition policy for the Center for Science in the Public Interest.[29]

Advertising works for food companies, who spend an estimated $13 billion a year on ads aimed at youth. A Public Health Institute survey of 12- to 17-year-olds found that 68 percent consume two or more servings a day of high-fat, low-nutrition foods, such as fried foods, candy, or soda.[30] Added fat and sugar contribute about half of the calories consumed by the average U.S. child. In recent years, the balance shifted and children now drink more soft drinks than milk.

A recent study found that grade-school kids drink an average of one can of soda a day. The researchers found that children who drink the most soda were less likely to eat fruits and vegetables.[31] Experts also say unhealthy diets contribute to growing weight problems among U.S. kids. In fact, 25 percent of U.S. children are overweight or at risk for obesity. Incredibly, these figures have more than doubled in just one generation.[32]

Obesity puts young people at risk for a variety of health problems. According to the Centers for Disease Control, 60 percent of overweight children have at least one risk factor for heart disease, including elevated blood pressure, cholesterol, and insulin levels. These are also the factors that lead to hypertension and diabetes.[33]

Perhaps it is not surprising that the incidence of obesity was highest among children who watched four or more hours of television a day and lowest among children who watched an hour or less a day.[34]

Fashion

Then. Aside from Levi's, the new specialized sports shoes, and a brief obsession with Earth Shoes, clothing for young people was downright generic.

Now. Check out the average young person's closet and dresser. You'll find designer sports shoes, a collection of dress shoes, a stack of jeans plus more pants, more shirts, more sweaters, and more jackets than ever before. At every age, kids have also upgraded to higher quality, more expensive clothing.

Brands Rule

Remember when clothing departments used to be organized by item—pants in one section and sweaters in another? Today they are most often organized by brand—Ralph Lauren here, DKNY over there.

And while young people today overwhelmingly prefer brand name apparel, many parents are right there supporting their kids' brand buying ways. According to BKG Youth, 64 percent of parents said it is important for their kids to wear status brands. Perhaps not surprisingly, 77 percent of children agree.[35]

With kids willing to serve as walking billboards for their favorite brands, manufacturers expend their design creativity on ways to emblazon their brand name logo—across the chest, across the back, along the sleeve, on a pocket, on a tab, engraved in the sole. The kids buy the clothing and proudly wear their badges of acceptance.

But as you will notice in the following list, as kids' preferences change, so, too, will their preferred brands. Note that only one of the five carried over from 1996 to 2002.

The Coolest Brands among Teens

2002	1996
1. Nike	1. Nike
2. Sony	2. Guess
3. Adidas	3. Levi's
4. Abercrombie & Fitch	4. Sega
5. Old Navy	5. Reebok

Source: Teenage Research Unlimited.

Brand loyalty comes at a price. Any parent whose child has upgraded to a branded wardrobe of Abercrombie & Fitch jeans, Tommy Hilfiger shirts, and Doc Marten shoes knows these items can run double or triple the cost of an anonymous equivalent.

Meanwhile, manufacturers do all they can to ingrain brand allure. Companies pay for product placements in movies and TV shows, usually for a fleeting moment on the screen as part of the environment of a scene. J. Crew arranged to dress the cast of the popular TV show, "Dawson's Creek," in the clothes sold in its catalog and stores.[36] What a coup to intertwine its brand with characters idolized by a faithful share of America's youth.

One of the great licensing success stories of the 1990s and the new millennium has to be the Olsen Twins. Mary-Kate and Ashley are not just teenage girls—they are a brand, like Legos or Cheerios. They are a cartoon, a doll, a web site, a line of clothing, accessories and cosmetics, a computer game, a series of books with more than 100 titles, a magazine, a music album, and a video.[37]

Going Tribal

Far from a homogenous group, teens actually represent a variety of subcultures, many of which have their own style and brands that specialize in that style. Consider the Vans brand. It is the ultracool line of clothes, shoes, and accessories for kids who skateboard and snowboard. There are Vans skateparks, concert tours, and events broadcast by NBC and FOX. Vans also partners with punk bands like Millencolin and then releases limited edition Millencolin shoes available only on their web site.[38]

As far as teens are concerned, Teenage Research Unlimited says brands are all about affiliation. In a way, youth fashion resembles tribal costumes. Certain clothes signal that you belong to a particular tribe and that you share the same interests and stand for the same things as the rest of the tribe. Not surprisingly, Forrester Research found that two-thirds of teens say they buy brands that reflect their style and they use brands to fashion an image for themselves.[39] In other words, you are what you wear. And nothing says that more clearly than the brands that pitch to your subculture.

Age Compression

In a classic marketing scenario, a company grows by capturing a larger slice of the pie or by creating a larger pie. The fashion world has expanded the pie by making fashion important at younger and younger ages. Knowing that children pay close attention to older kids and often emulate them, fashion companies have succeeded in making children want what they have to sell. Teen girls spend $33 billion a year on fashion and beauty, says *Seventeen*, and cosmetics companies eagerly welcome billions more from preteen girls.[40]

For the last five years, children's fashions have been the fastest-growing category of apparel. Children's wear departments and specialty stores have sprouted quickly throughout the nation. Gap Kids, Abercrombie, and Limited Too are just a few of the stores that nurture brand awareness among youngsters and entice them to dress like the big kids.

Some parents dress their children in designer clothing even before the children are conscious of fashion. Upscale department stores offer clothes from Ralph Lauren, Tommy Hilfiger, DKNY, and others in toddler sizes. The early years offer the best chance to save on the price of kids' clothing, and yet the trend toward high-end children's wear means that a 2T can mirror the style and the price of adult clothes.

Music

Then. Music blasted from unsophisticated car speakers and from the family's hi-fi or a working teen's own stereo system. Once a week, you might turn on "American Bandstand" to see kids your age dance to the Top 40 or catch rock bands performing their latest hits on "The Midnight Special."

Now. Teens in pursuit of perfect sound frequently upgrade their boombox, replace the original CD player and speakers in the car, and buy the latest technology. To revitalize its Walkman brand and expand it to digital music, Sony linked Walkman to the younger generation's way of life through an integrated marketing campaign that incorporated television, print, product placement, online content, and event marketing. Sony jumped to number one in sales of portable digital players even though the company boosted average prices to an 85 percent premium over the rest of the industry.[41] By no coincidence, the coolest brands also have some of the biggest teen marketing budgets.

Music Sells

The emotional bond between young people and their music provides endless opportunities for companies to ride the coattails of popular music, Today there are two key differences from 1970: product placement and points of contact.

In product placement, companies seek out kid-friendly musicians to build the credibility of their brands. Pepsi, one of the early adopters of this strategy, has heavily promoted its alliance with Britney Spears in a series of commercials that resemble music videos.

Radio Disney and Nickelodeon have presented their own music festivals. Levi's jeans and Sears Roebuck and Co. sponsored a 37-city tour by singer Christina Aguilera. Hot Topic, a retailer for teen girls, and the Vans footwear company also have sponsored teen-oriented concert tours. Guess what? The performers often wear the sponsors' products on stage.

In 2000, McDonald's discovered that music can rekindle older kids' desire to eat there after they've outgrown Happy Meals. A promotion featuring a CD and video from Britney Spears and *NSYNC produced a healthy sales increase for McDonald's. Not your typical giveaway, the CD brought in young customers who ordered a meal and paid an additional $4.99 for the CD. Burger King soon followed with a Backstreet Boys CD that cost $2.99 with the purchase of a Value Meal. Burger King referred to the promotion as its first attempt to target the tween market. Expect more of these pop-star promotions. They're good business for the record companies, which get distribution, and the restaurants, which lure customers.[42]

45

I Want My MTV

The second key difference from 1970 is points of contact. Take a close look at MTV, the global godfather of youth-oriented music. MTV transformed the industry by making music a medium for the ears and the eyes. More than that, MTV has intertwined music and lifestyle. It embodies 24-hour marketing. MTV programming essentially presents one big infomercial that tells young people what music they should listen to, what clothes they should wear, and what other products they should buy to keep up with the MTV-endorsed lifestyle. Remember, MTV is in business to sell advertising, and it can sell more ads at a higher price by getting results for its advertisers.

Consider the enormous success of MTV's *Total Request Live*. The show, which airs weekdays, is all about building hype for different bands and their music. Whether it's an up close and personal interview with a band that's in the MTV studio or encouraging viewers to vote for their favorite video online, the goal is the same. Buy the culture, buy the music, and buy the products. Some parents might argue that the "M" stands for manipulate.

Communication

Then. You stayed in touch with friends by phone. Your home probably had one phone line. For convenience and occasional privacy, you may have had an extra phone or two plugged into a phone jack.

Now. The home phone is just one option for communicating with friends. With a separate kids' phone line, pagers, cell phones, instant messaging, chat rooms, and e-mail, your children and their friends can reach each other any time, anywhere. In a survey of 13- to 24-year-olds, the Zandl Group found that 84 percent have an e-mail account, and 49 percent have a cell phone.[43]

46

The Mobile Generation

Experts predict that the current explosion of communication technology will shape today's youth much the same way that television shaped your generation. As the first children to use pagers and cellular phones, they have adopted this technology as their own and made it central to their lifestyle, prompting researchers to dub them the Mobile Generation. Teens have become the fastest-growing market for cell phones, and telecommunications companies want their business.

The Façade of Control

The growing list of phone capabilities gives kids tremendous power to control communication. A separate kids' line eliminates the need to set time limits on calls and lessens the need for siblings to share the phone. With portable phones, they gain the freedom to roam about the house and yard while on a call. With call waiting, they avoid missing a call to a busy signal and conduct the next best thing to a conference call. With caller ID, they screen calls and choose which ones to answer. With pagers, they and their friends can be reached away from home. And with cell phones and instant messaging, they can "talk" with friends wherever they are.

Despite the increased ability to stay in touch, each gain in technology seems to have heightened the urgency of communication for today's youth. Making plans on a weekend night can become frantic with the home phone, kids' phone, cell phone and maybe a pager ringing or buzzing and your child scrambling to avoid the trauma of a missed call.

Whether or not phone companies understood teen thinking when they developed some of their services, the fact is that their pricing exploits kids' urgent need to stay in touch. Kids didn't know what they were missing before the introduction of *69, which is dialed to identify a missed call. Now that they know about it, kids dial it often, even though it carries a hefty charge with each use. Likewise, entry-level plans for cell phones include a modest number of minutes for day-time calls. Even after exceeding the limit, kids often keep making and receiving calls, choosing to talk now and pay extra charges later.

Techno Chic

In a matter of a few years, the cell phone has become a cul-tural icon for those who are young, popular, and on the go. *The Wall Street Journal* calls cell phones a "teen status sym-bol—the BMW Roadster for the under-20 set."[44]

More than just a technological device, the cell phone makes a fashion statement. Getting the right brand marks the starting point. From there, phone companies and manu-facturers encourage teens to personalize their phones. Some teens use multiple interchangeable faceplates to change their phones to match their mood or outfit.

Now consumer-product companies have joined forces with technology companies to build sales for phone fash-ions. In a joint venture with teen cosmetic company Hard Candy, Motorola offers interchangeable colored and tex-tured covers for its wireless phones in Hard Candy nail-pol-ish colors. Companies like Disney, which sells phones decorated with Disney characters, target the tween market.[45]

A New Way to Communicate

Now that nearly all schools in the United States have com-puters and 70 percent of households with children have a computer, most kids have access to the Internet and e-mail—one more technology for communicating with each other.[46]

As a form of written communication, e-mail gives your

child a chance to think over and revise the messages he or she sends to others. In a survey of kids age 10 to 17, more than one-third said they feel more "popular and outgoing" online. Nearly seven out of ten said it's easier to express what they believe on the Internet than in person. They also feel smart when they use the Internet.[47]

As a tool for seeking information, the Internet gives kids the power to visit web sites for organizations around the world. Virtually every company and brand with products for kids has a web site designed especially for kids. On the surface, these sites offer interactive games and other activities that simply entertain or even educate. But the underlying motive never wavers. The company wants to develop a relationship with your child in hopes of nurturing long-term loyalty and sales.

Consider the story of Vans, the ultrahip retailer of shoes, clothing, and snowboarding accessories. I sold Vans sneakers in high school in the early '80s. At that time, Vans was mostly geared toward skateboarding. Today, Vans uses an e-mail distribution service to send customers messages offering limited-edition sneakers. A 2000 promotion targeted young women for its Compel shoe, which changes color when exposed to the sun. An e-mail included a 3-D rotating picture of the sneaker changing color and a promise that the first batch was being saved for online customers.[48]

Shopping

Then. Shopping was drudgery, a necessary evil that often involved multiple stops. Ten years after the nation's first enclosed shopping center opened in 1960, the best shopping in most cities was still downtown, which meant hassles taking a bus or finding a place to park. Worse yet, you probably bought your clothes from the same stores as your parents. If you couldn't find what you wanted in a department store, you could always order from the Sears catalog.

Now. Shopping represents entertainment, convenience, and global access. In enormous suburban malls filled with department stores, specialty shops, movie theaters, and food courts, just about anything your kids want can be found under one roof. And don't forget the 24-7 shopping extravaganza available on the Internet.

Starting Young

Most children make their first independent purchase at a convenience store. By the time they reach their teens, nearly 75 percent of American youths make at least one trip per week—a collective 100 million trips per month—to a convenience store.[49] To give young children an early lesson in shopping, Southland Corporation's 7-Eleven stores in 2000 established a toy section. Their strategy: Give kids the products they want when they are young, and they'll keep coming back in the future. The 7-Eleven chain of 20,000 stores now carries teen items like body jewelry, hair accessories, and CDs.[50]

Discount stores, a common destination for young families, have staying power with young people, too. When asked what kind of store they shopped at in the last 30 days, the number one answer among teens was a discount store, such as Target or Wal-Mart. Target clearly calls for the youth dollar with music-video-style commercials populated by young adults.[51]

Mall Appeal

Shopping the mall has become a ritual of the American lifestyle, performed 54 times a year by the average teen.[52] The Mall of America, the nation's largest enclosed shopping mall, opened in Bloomington, Minnesota, in 1992. In its first ten years, over 270 million people—as many as 900,000 a week—visited the mall with its 520 stores in 4.2 million square feet of space. Aside from shopping, the key attractions include Camp Snoopy, an indoor amusement park; Underwater Adventures, an aquarium; and Lego Imagination Center, an area where kids can build to their hearts' content with an enormous supply of Lego parts. All focused on young children, these attractions teach kids that shopping centers are fun and even a great place to have a birthday party.[53]

In a 1997 study for the National Park Service, the Mall of America ranked as the most visited destination for U.S. travelers. In a study on brand awareness, the Mall of America ranked ahead of GE, one of the country's largest, most successful and most respected companies. According to their web site, the mall plans to build an additional 5 million square feet of space.[54]

To increase their drawing power with young people, some malls have created youth zones. The Glendale Galleria, in suburban Los Angeles, discovered that teens spend a yearly average of $2700 apiece at the mall.[55] To make it an even more inviting destination, the Galleria opened The Zone, a section featuring a cluster of teen-oriented stores and a teens-only lounge area with a DJ, large-screen TVs, and Internet kiosks.[56]

For Youth Only

Specialized stores that cater to the youth market now fill the roster of mall tenants. With shopping for clothes ranked as the top mall activity among teens and tweens, according to Roper Youth Report 2000, clothing retailers have led the quest for youth dollars. Openings of specialty-apparel stores aimed at young people are growing 17 percent a year—more than double the overall rate of the specialty-apparel sector. "The kids' field is exploding these days," said Robert D. Riedy, CLS, vice president at The Rouse Co., which manages shopping malls.[57]

Gap, The Limited, J. Crew, and Abercrombie & Fitch give teens and young adults a place they can call their own, although many parents shop there, too. Now retailers are getting more specialized to target slices of the highly segmented youth market and move kids into more expensive clothing at a younger age. Often an offshoot of an established retailer, these new stores focus on a particular style or niche or a narrow age group. "When I was growing up in Connecticut, there weren't teen retailers," says Greg Weaver, chairman and CEO of Pacific Sunwear, a California-based chain that sells surfer fashions to teens.[58]

In the spirit of age compression, Gap Kids, Limited Too, and just plain Abercrombie go after preteens. Boo Girls, Curiouser & Curiouser, Time Goes By, and Star-Spangled Carousel cater to tween girls.

New Retail Chains in Youth Niches[59]

Chain	Parent Company	Specialty
Hollister Co.	Abercrombie & Fitch	Surfer and skateboarder fashions for ages 7 to 14
Velvet Pixies	Claire's Stores	Name-brand clothes for preteen girls
Torrid	Hot Topic	Trendy clothes for large-size girls age 15 and up
Mishmash	Limited Too	Shoes, cosmetics, and intimate apparel for girls who outgrow Limited Too
D.e.m.o.	Pacific Sunwear	Urban, industrial, and ethnic fashions for teens

Meanwhile, specialty retailers in other categories have developed their own youth concepts. For example, now you can find home furnishings with kid appeal at Pottery Barn for Kids.

Another hit at malls, Build-A-Bear Workshop invites children of all ages to make a customized teddy bear. To keep up the relationship, the store sends a birthday card on the anniversary of each bear's purchase and invites customers to bring their bears back for refurbishing on a free "spa day."

Of course, department stores and discount stores want part of the action, too. Sears featured a Christina Aguilera-themed area and offered Aguilera CDs made especially for Sears, a sponsor of her concert tour. Target has established a section of fun furnishings for teen and preteen bedrooms.

Others with an interest in youth spending also see opportunity. In a licensing agreement, *Seventeen* magazine and Teen Studios plan to open a Seventeen Studio/Spa/Salon in Dallas. The shop targets female teens with hair services, manicures, pedicures, professional makeup instruction, teen facials, waxing, and massage services.[60]

Instant Access

The Internet takes immediate gratification to a whole new level. A child with a computer and Internet service has instant access to global shopping. It may be the web site for a chain with a local store, a retailer in another state or another country, or the manufacturer. No waiting for Mom or Dad or a friend for a ride to the mall. No driving time. Just a couple clicks, and you're in a virtual store. By 2005, estimates suggest, kids will spend $4.9 billion online, with Web-influenced sales of $21 billion.[61]

TOP PRODUCTS PURCHASED BY TEENS ONLINE

1. CDs/Cassettes
2. Clothing
3. Books
4. Computer software
5. Toys

Source: PricewaterhouseCoopers.

For kids, surfing the Web is entertainment. For commercial web sites, each visit represents a chance to build a relationship with the child and ultimately make a sale. So, whether your child is shopping or playing a game, the undercurrents sweep them toward making or influencing a purchase.

Virtual Malls

A new breed of web site creates youth communities that act as virtual malls, where kids hang out with their friends, chat, and do some shopping. Sites like bolt.com, alloy.com, and gurl.com offer edgy content and loads of product information in a highly interactive format. Some say the sites act as computer-powered teen magazines. That explains why magazines like *Seventeen, Teen People, YM, Teen,* and *Cosmo Girl* developed their own youth community sites.

The sites draw kids for the social gathering, and the brands want to be where kids spend time. When you peer below the sense of community, these sites have two things in common: feeding the urge to buy and giving companies access to young people.

"It doesn't make a difference if you close a sale online or offline. The key is having that person in your circle of assets," says Matt Diamond, CEO of Alloy, Inc., a media and marketing services company whose site focuses on young people ages 10 to 24.[62]

Funny Money

New products from financial service companies help kids spend their money. A sponsored debit card from organizations like Visa and American Express looks like a credit card and works like a credit card. But Visa and American Express swear it's not a credit card. No, they say it's a convenience for parents who don't want to be a walking, talking ATM for their kids. And, they say, it's a tool for teaching your child money management. For the target market of kids age 13 and up, the important thing is that it lets a kid charge purchases online, charge purchases at countless stores, and get cash from an ATM.[63]

With PocketCard, Visa Buxx, CobaltCard, and M2card (short for mobile money), each transaction draws on an account with a set limit, similar to a prepaid phone card. Parents replenish the account by transferring funds from a credit card or bank account. You can even set up regular transfers as an allowance. Parents track their child's use of the card through daily e-mail updates, visits to the card's web site, and monthly financial statements.

The card companies refer to the card as training wheels. They say it offers protection because the child can't spend or withdraw any more than the card's limit. In truth, it's a learner's permit for a credit card. Your child gets to practice, practice, practice—hitting the ATM, buying stuff the moment the urge strikes, using plastic like play money. Rest assured the kids with a sponsored debit card will be among the first to get their own credit card.

Cautioning against debit cards, author Neale S. Godfrey

says kids first need basic lessons on how to handle money. "You just don't hand the keys to the car to a child without driver's education, and you don't hand a financial vehicle to a child without financial education," she says.[64]

Janet Bodnar, author of *Dollars and Sense for Kids*, agrees that kids need experience managing hard currency before they touch plastic: "Plastic is very abstract. With plastic, it's very difficult for kids to grasp the idea they're actually spending money because nothing is changing hands. They still don't have the idea of money being subtracted from an account, and the only way they're going to get that is through the concrete experience of spending actual cash money."[65]

Beyond the issue of handling money, debit cards promote a habit of spending. Repetition is an effective teacher. Make enough stops at the cash machine, make enough purchases with plastic, and they become part of your being. Credit card companies want their card in your child's pocket at a young age, so they can start banking on a lifetime of consumer habits. Give your child a debit card, and you fast forward to a state of illusion, where make-believe money leads to a mountain of consumer debt.

Web sites actually pioneered teen debit accounts as part of their strategy to kick-start electronic commerce. Although they target different segments of the under-18 market, RocketCash and PocketCard enable kids to shop online without a credit card. These "digital wallet" accounts are no better than debit cards and may be more habit-forming. Wandering around a virtual mall at their fingertips, kids can spend faster than they possibly could in person.

Whether it's a plastic card or an online account, teen debit plans do nothing more than feed the greed of our consumer culture. That spells opportunity for all kinds of businesses. Last year, Coca-Cola was so pleased with an under-the-cap promotion involving RocketCash and its Sprite brand that it bought RocketCash.

Money Talks

- How does the home you grew up in compare to your home today in number of bedrooms, bathrooms, and garage stalls, closet space, appliances, and electronics?
- How do your child's toys compare to the toys you had as a child?
- How often and why did your family eat out when you were a child? Where? Why?
- How does your child's wardrobe compare to yours at the same age?
- How do your child's options for music compare to those you had at the same age?
- In what ways is communication with friends the same for your child as it was for you at the same age? In what ways is it different?
- How do your child's favorite shopping destinations differ from the places you shopped at the same age?

Chapter FOUR

The Teen Commandments

Attitudes that stimulate spending by young people start to develop at a young age. They are shaped by advertising, crafty marketing tactics, television, movies, peer pressure, parental actions and assorted social experiences. Like Ravel's *Bolero*, from the soundtrack of the movie *10*, these influences start softly but steadily build until the entire orchestra plays the throbbing rhythm of consumerism. As a result, most kids start moving to the tempo and eventually adopt an upscale lifestyle.

By the teen years, these attitudes are so much a part of America's youth that they border on religion. Because the power of these attitudes approaches biblical proportions, let's call them the Teen Commandments. Just as the original Ten Commandments provided a guide for living, the Teen Commandments instruct young people on a new way of life.

These attitudes are exactly what trouble parents. At many of my workshops, concerned parents across the United States consistently describe examples of increasing selfishness, inflated expectations, and disregard for consequences in their children's behavior. Some attitudes impart strong financial overtones on common themes of adolescence. Others illustrate greed, eroding values, a shaky sense of self-worth, and the enormous power of marketing. Like it or not, the following are the commandments that create today's mutant version of the American Dream.

1. Nag, and You Shall Receive.

The incessant nag factor must be working because kids have more influence over parents' purchases than ever before. It may start small—with a piece of candy, then a small toy, then the latest tennis shoes. Look out! In the blink of an eye, you'll be arranging a loan at a car dealership while junior waits impatiently behind the wheel of his new automobile.

Young people have always pestered their parents for things they want. So what's different today? Two big factors: time and money. Parents have so little time to spend with their kids that they spend more money on their kids to make up for the lack of time.

In stores all across the country, tired parents issue the standard statement of surrender: "Oh, all right." It beats the alternative—whining, stomping, crying, and screaming. At the end of a busy day or in the midst of a hectic weekend, many parents are willing to part with a few bucks to avoid the abuse and embarrassment of a child's tantrum. The fact that parents give in more often now encourages kids to nag even more.

Sarah says her 8-year-old son has the nag down to a science. "He studies the situation very carefully before he starts in on his request," said Sarah. He considers the price, Mom's mood, and other factors. "Sometimes I wonder if he and his little friends at school plot their strategy on how to wear down Mom or Dad."

2. Wait Not for What You Want.

When you live for the moment, you don't worry about consequences. Immediate gratification is too seductive to ignore. That's why convenience is so irresistible to this generation, why they're an easy mark for offers to buy now and pay later, and why kids with metered service on a cell phone keep talking even after they exceed their allocation of free minutes. When you grow up knowing that every consumer need can be fulfilled with one click on a web site, what else should a young person think?

Doug, a recent college graduate, admits to falling into the trap of immediate gratification. "Everything you are bombarded with—commercials, advertising, and marketing—is geared toward impulse buying," he said. "When I was a kid, I would borrow money from my brother just to buy little things that I had to have that day. At 22, I still buy things I know I shouldn't."

When he bought a car, Doug spent more than he should have, but the process made it easy. "As hard as I try, it's tough to keep that discipline and say no to things you want," said Doug, who works two jobs to maintain his lifestyle.

3. Only the Best Will Do.

When you expect the best, riding in a $30,000 minivan is so embarrassing. Expecting the best means paying more for everything from skateboards to stereo speakers. It means upgrading the computer, video game console or car stereo—even if it still works—when a new, improved version becomes available.

Imagine your child's reaction if you said this year's vacation would be spent in a tent at a nearby state park. If friends' families plan to jet off to trendy places for their annual getaway, you'll hear about it.

Sean, 41, contrasts his trip to Disneyland in California as a kid (circa 1973) with the trip he and his wife and their three boys, ages 3, 6, and 7, recently made to Disney World in Orlando, Florida. "When I was a kid, we loaded six people and all our stuff for two weeks in the family sedan and made the 3000-plus-mile round-trip from Wisconsin to California," he recalled. Along the way, they stayed in cheap motels, where they all shared one room.

"This year," he said, "the five of us plus two grandparents flew to Florida, where we rented a four-bedroom, three-bathroom house complete with swimming pool and cable TV for all three TVs, plus one minivan and a car."

4. Fit in at All Costs.

When acceptance requires wearing the right brand of jeans, shirts, and athletic shoes, kids don't just ask for a certain brand, they insist that their very existence depends on it.

Teens' obsession with brand names traces directly to their deep desire to fit in with their peers. Wearing the latest label announces to the world that he or she belongs. It's no coincidence that many teen boys wear clothes from Abercrombie & Fitch and that just about every kid has at least one pair of Nikes. Because they calibrate themselves and their possessions against those of their peers, kids often resemble mirror images of their friends.

Rachel, a 39-year-old single mom, described how her daughter, Jenny, came home dejected after her first week in seventh grade. "She told me that *all* her friends had much cooler clothes and that she couldn't possibly go back to school on Monday unless we went shopping over the weekend," Rachel said. What followed was a difficult conversation about life as a single parent and how she couldn't afford to buy the popular brands. But that wasn't going to stop Jenny.

"She ended up borrowing money from a friend and begging her dad to buy her 'just a couple of things,'" Rachel said. Since the divorce two years ago, Jenny has perfected the art of playing the pity card with her father.

5. Grow Up As Fast As You Can.

With today's kids, you're never as old as you want to be. According to Teenage Research Unlimited, most 12-year-olds aspire to be 17-year-olds. Age compression is everywhere. Whether it's provocative clothes, makeup, or a TV for your bedroom, these milestones occur at younger and younger ages.

The fact is that consumer goods companies and retailers encourage kids to dress older. For example, manufacturers produce and retailers sell low-cut tops and low-riding pants to fit preteen girls so they can dress like sexy pop stars Britney Spears and Christina Aguilera. *The Wall Street Journal* reported that teen girls have boosted the market for brightly colored and skimpy lingerie. Now that more teen girls wear padded bras and push-up bras, they've made Victoria's Secret one of their favorite brands.[1]

Joan's oldest daughter, Stephanie, was 12 when she asked for new underwear and said she wanted to go to Victoria's Secret, like her friend Katy does. Joan decided to call Katy's mother to get more information. "She told me she took Katy and Stephanie to Victoria's Secret when they went shopping at the mall," Joan recalled. "She said their stuff really only looks good on young girls because they have the perfect bodies. I told her how disappointed I was with her comments and that Stephanie was too young for that shop."

Meanwhile, most of the girls in her youngest daughter's fourth-grade class wear makeup. "My daughter and a few others are the exception," Joan said. "I let her wear lip gloss, but that's it." Even Barbie, the doll from Mattel, has her own line of 40 beauty products—from bath and body to nail colors and lip shimmers—just for young girls.

6. When It's Special, Make It Extravagant.

When competition meets a heightened sense of importance, you find a fertile climate for extravagance. Many kids have the notion that every birthday, event, and milestone must be better than the last. No expense is too great for a special occasion. How about renting a full-size Barbie car, having an overnight in FAO Schwarz, or renting ponies for the backyard party? If you think it can't possibly get any more decadent, check out the kids getting picked up in a limo on the day they "graduate" from sixth grade. And don't forget the high school girls who spend $250 or more for a dress they'll wear one night at the prom.

Tim was surprised by the birthday party his 14-year-old daughter, Trisha, attended: "The theme was 'a day of beauty and fun.' Let me tell you, it was like no birthday party I ever attended." The party started with a visit to a local spa, where each girl received a mini-facial, a manicure, and a makeup application. Then a limousine took them to the mall, where each girl had a gift certificate to buy something for the dance that evening. "It was incredible," Tim said. "Apparently, the girl's parents hired a DJ and rented a room at the local country club for 50 of her closest friends."

7. More Is Better.

If you want it all and get it, you never have to share or compromise. The cornerstone of excess, this commandment makes it vital to have one of your own—your own phone, your own TV and VCR, your own boombox, even your own computer.

With some things, one is not enough, certainly not when it comes to Beanie Babies, video games, caps, jeans, and black platform shoes. For further proof, look inside your child's bedroom or playroom.

Chris, a 16-year-old technophile, has a bedroom that could double as a showroom for one of the leading electronics retailers. He has a big-screen TV, VCR, DVD player, surround-sound stereo, computer with all the latest gear, a printer/fax/scanner/copier, lots of video games, his own telephone line, and a cell phone. Chris almost glows when describing his collection of more than 300 CDs and DVDs, but his most telling comment smacks of envy: "If you think I have a great collection, you should see my friend Jason's."

8. You Are Entitled to What You Want.

Kids seem to believe they deserve whatever they want, whenever they want it. This sense of entitlement is the driving force behind the nag factor. One mother said her older daughter once stated, "If I want something, and you have the money, I should get it."

When you insist on whatever is just right for you, you fight for your preference. For example, now that Red Lobster, Outback Steakhouse, and Olive Garden rank among their favorite restaurants, teens often argue for their choice and against the parents' preference for a less expensive option.[2]

Valerie couldn't understand why she didn't get the exact bike she wanted for her eighth birthday. "Valerie blamed my husband and me for not trying harder to find the bike we knew she wanted," said her mother, Gretchen.

"She said we drove all over town looking for her older brother Danny's skateboard, and she couldn't understand why we didn't do the same for her." The parents felt they had to comply.

9. Pursue the "Perfect" You.

Living in a society that obsesses on appearance, many teens strive for some elusive image of perfection. Because others are watching and judging, they buy tans, hair colors, hairstyles, manicured nails, and more. Insecurity reigns. If you can never be satisfied with your physical appearance, you forever search for possible improvements. And, in the relentless pursuit of perfection, consequences take a back seat.

Consider tanning beds. Young people flock to tanning salons to jumpstart a bronzed look in preparation for summer vacation or a spring break trip or to preserve that August skin tone in January. While research from the likes of Dartmouth Medical School shows that tanning bed exposure increases the risk for skin cancer, 51 percent of high-school-age girls in the United States use a tanning bed at least four times a year.[3]

To control their weight, some young people buy diet pills, laxatives, and diuretics. To bulk up, the National Institute of Drug Abuse estimates, as many as 325,000 teenage boys use steroids.[4] To correct a perceived flaw, a growing number of young people resort to plastic surgery. According to the American Society for Aesthetic Plastic Surgery, nearly 300,000 people under age 18 underwent an elective procedure in 2001.[5] Nose reshaping ranks as the most common procedure. A new area of growth: calf implants for a more muscled and sculpted look in young males.

Janet recalls her decision to use diet pills as a teenager.

"I really wanted to be skinnier in high school and turned to diet pills as the quick fix. I desperately wanted to be thin like some of my girlfriends," she said. At 32, Janet worries that girls today have even more pressure to look thin and beautiful. "I cringe when I see what young people are doing to improve their physical appearance," she said. "Unfortunately, it seems to be getting worse instead of better."

10. Forget Reality.

A high school student needs his own car because "Nobody rides the bus. The bus is for losers." A high school senior needs to go to Mexico for spring break because "Everyone else is going." A college student gets a credit card and racks up a balance on essentials: travel, restaurants, and bars. When a self-absorbed teen wants something, logic vanishes. Pay no attention to the cost or the ability to pay.

The epitome of narcissism, many teens believe that others notice every detail about them. They constantly need new clothes to avoid being accused of wearing the same thing more than an acceptable limit. Because every call is too important to be interrupted, they talk on a cell phone while seated next to the home phone. All these choices carry a price tag, but money is no object when their image and their convenience are on the line.

Consider the situation of a young man who was in private school in suburban Minneapolis. Early in his senior year, his family fell behind on tuition payments. The school established a reasonable payback schedule which included the young man working off some of the debt. But rather than comply with the mutual agreement, the young man chose to go on a spring break trip with his friends. He claims to have "needed a break."

The school responded by stating he wouldn't be allowed to graduate with his class because he hadn't lived up to his end of the agreement. Outraged, his fellow classmates held a fund-raiser to bail him out. They couldn't believe the school would be so cruel.

The Fate of Generosity

The Teen Commandments pose a fundamental question: Is this new way of life simply an adolescent phase that eventually passes, or will it continue into adulthood?

I fear that a generation focused on itself might fail to respond to societal needs. In the past, Americans grew up with altruistic values like caring for others, aiding those in need, and helping people who are less fortunate. Reaching out to others in time of need is a longstanding component of the American way. What will come of this outward focus if millions of young people skew toward self-indulgence?

Today's young people already wield access and influence over a tremendous amount of cash. The collective impact of Generation Y—a group equal to nearly one-third of the U.S. population—will resonate for decades to come. But what can be expected from a generation brainwashed by the relentless voice of the consumer culture? Corporate America strategically drowns out traditional values with seductive and persuasive campaigns that celebrate serving self. In effect, corporate America penned the Teen Comandments to reap the rewards of wooing this well-financed generation.

A self-centered generation carries a dire price for society. What happens if this generation, in its prime earning years, is too preoccupied with buying bigger and better stuff to notice that the Red Cross, United Way, and other causes need donations? What if they have the desire to help but don't have the means because they're deep in debt?

Money Talks

- Which commandments do you see in other adults?
- Which commandments do you see in yourself?
- Which commandments does your child see in other young people?
- Which commandments does your child see in himself or herself?

Chapter FIVE

The Three-Headed Monster

In the game of chess, two willing participants engage in a battle of strategic positioning. The outcome largely depends on each player's anticipation of the opponent's moves. As the game progresses, the players capture more and more pieces. The winner corners the opponent's king and finally declares, "Checkmate." If you've ever played chess, winning can be quite satisfying. And, depending on the skill level of the players, the game can last for hours, even days.

Consumer goods companies play chess with America's children in a covert game that lasts for years. They invest billions of dollars a year to anticipate what children think and do, then strategically position their resources to spur kids to move around the board, chasing the latest fad or trend. In fact, most major companies that target young people employ such sophisticated marketing techniques that each year they move closer and closer to absolute knowledge of children's every move. When kids don't even know they're playing, what are the odds they won't be captured?

"Katie is an intelligent, confident, value-centered young

person," Sarah said of her 15-year-old daughter. "One day she was laughing at how some kids at school were 'ruled' by their brand loyalty, and the following week she was begging me to take her shopping for a specific type of clothing." Sarah believes some message finally convinced her daughter that she wouldn't fit in if she didn't wear that specific brand. Checkmate.

The mastermind behind this mismatch may best be described as a three-headed monster—a high-powered triumvirate of consumer-products companies, media conglomerates, and advertising agencies. Together they scheme to shape the consumer habits of young people by creating a tangled web of money, manipulation, and influence. Doing business in a virtually lawless arena, they stop at nothing as they compete for shares of a child's heart, mind, soul, and wallet.

The year 1992 was a turning point in youth marketing. Naomi Klein, author of *No Logo: Taking Aim at the Brand Bullies*, writes: "To understand how youth culture became such a sought-after market in the early nineties, it helps to go back to the recession era 'brand crisis' that took root immediately preceding this frenzy—a crisis that, with so many consumers failing to live up to corporate expectations, created a clear and pressing need for a new class of shoppers to step in and take over." When companies realized that beer, soft drinks, fast food, sneakers, chewing gum, and Barbie dolls were among the items that flourished during the recession, they took aim at a new target.[1]

The three-headed monster continually attempts to eliminate consumer restraint and fiscal responsibility from our value system. Never before have such incredible resources been devoted to shaping the financial values of an entire generation. In this campaign without a conscience, the goal is to warp your children's perspective of needs and wants, to put them under a hypnotic spell of spending that could last a lifetime.

Beware, parents. These companies are monsters in scale

and in actions. They prey on children, pushing products with little regard for children's welfare and exploiting children's every weakness. They are predators, and their tactics of manipulation and seduction border on child abuse.

Consumer Product Companies

Through countless hours of research and an enormous financial investment, Procter & Gamble (P&G) recently discovered a new marketing technique called social network marketing. Using local teenagers who are popular and vocal to spread the word on its products, P&G has created "the new gold standard for influencing kids," said Steve Knox, vice president of Business Development.[2]

Here's how it works. P&G, maker of CoverGirl, Max Factor, Clairol, Pantene, Tampax, Noxzema and other health-and-beauty products, locates so-called connectors—teens with broad social networks and an interest in "discovering and telling others about relevant new ideas." Procter & Gamble estimates this elite population at 8 to 10 percent of teens. They then leak information to the connectors and its custom grapevine goes to work.[3]

Procter & Gamble conducted a market test of connectors in greater Knoxville, Tennessee, in May 2001. "We worked with some of the local TV affiliates to introduce a new all-day lipstick, and the results were beyond anything we expected," Knox said.[4]

Procter & Gamble sent connectors an e-mail with a folder attached and marked "Confidential: for your eyes only." The folder contained a script for the season finale of a popular TV show. Around the same time, P&G sent the connectors a product sample for the new lipstick, which would be advertised during the show. One subtle twist: P&G blacked out lines on the script so the connectors wouldn't know how the show ended.[5]

The connectors told their friends about their advance knowledge of the finale and the cool, new product. When the test was complete, P&G discovered that local ratings for the episode were triple that of the same week in May 2000. The share of teens tuning in for the season finale went from 21.9 in May 2000 to 38.9 in May 2001—a remarkable increase that meant more potential customers received an introduction to P&G's new product. Voila! Product sales, according to Knox, jumped a double-digit percentage.[6] As clothing retailer Elise Decoteau said of teens, "They run in packs. If you sell to one, you sell to everyone in their class and everyone in their school."

Procter & Gamble identified 25,000 connectors across the country as of early 2002 and projected a network of 150,000 by year's end. Now Procter & Gamble, a $40-billion corporation with more than 300 brands and a budget upwards of $30 million for advertising just in teen magazines, has a new tool for pulling the strings of American youth.[7] This is the same Procter & Gamble that was voted the "#1 Best Corporate Citizen for 2001" by *Business Ethics* magazine.

When told about this marketing tactic, Kari, mother of a teen and a tween, sighed in disbelief: "We're pretty good about monitoring how much our kids are influenced by material possessions, but when it's so manipulative, I'm not sure what you can do."

Consumer product companies, including manufacturers, retailers, and services, develop and sell toys, clothes, snacks, movies, and other products designed to appeal to kids. To convince kids they want the products, these companies spend more than $230 billion a year in advertising, or $2190 per household, according to advertising giant McCann-Erickson. And there is little question that much of the advertising is designed to effectively target kids.[8]

Saturation is the art of pitching a product over and over wherever marketers can reach us. As much as possible, advertisers saturate our world with their messages in movies, on television, in magazines, on bathroom walls. They make it possible for the average child to see between 20,000 and 40,000 television commercials every year.[9] Advertisers will do anything to create a following for their product, and they concoct an endless stream of devious ways to plug their products.

Infecting Teens with Exoloopaphobia

Teens are so important to AT&T that the company launched a $100 million campaign targeting teens for their toll-free collect service. To crystallize its latest marketing strategy for targeting young people, AT&T Wireless invented the word *exo-loop-a-phobia*, defined by AT&T as the fear of being out of the loop. Knowing that cell phones are a key weapon in the teen's communication arsenal, AT&T Wireless plans to create anxiety and uneasiness in young people who don't have its product. The thinking goes that, without the appropriate electronic communication device, teens will feel left behind in the fast-paced world of communication.[10]

Ideas for this seductive campaign came from teens visiting a Disney theme park. While Mom and Dad were touring "The World of Innovation," the AT&T-sponsored sphere at Epcot Center, researchers lassoed teens for a focus group in a back room for their input on what the company's commercials should say.

Spies on the Street

To ease any hint of consumer distrust, companies try to make their campaigns more subtle and more local. Levi's, Coca-Cola, Pepsi, and Old Navy are among those using "street teams." The company plants teams of young people in clubs, parks, and malls so they can hang out and talk to teens about everything from fashion to finance. The goal is to detect trends as they emerge.[11]

Launching a Grassroots Campaign

Other companies try to build grassroots support for their brands. Some tack ad posters on street corners and construction sites. Some sponsor community events or hand out freebies at concerts. Golden Books Publishing Co. went to movie theaters to distribute sample chapters from a new teen book series. Coca-Cola went after the popular crowd first, mailing discount cards for movies and fast food to teens identified as high school sports stars and other leaders, then distributed more at stores, giving other kids a chance to feel included.

A Tangled Web

An estimated 55 percent of children's and teen's web sites feature games, which encourage kids to stay at a site longer. With many of these games, the company integrates products into the fun as a game piece or as hidden treasure.[12]

The Children's Online Privacy Protection Act of 2000 forbids selling to kids under age 13 via e-mail without parental permission. Web marketers invented viral campaigns to circumvent the law. They simply rely on kids to use e-mail to forward a marketing message to their friends, who forward it to their friends, and so on. For example, if your child goes to sesameworkshop.org and sends an electronic greeting card with a Sesame Street character, Elmo is likely to make the rounds.

Some companies go so far as to interact with kids at independent web sites. *BusinessWeek* reports that, when Tiger

Electronics, a division of Hasbro, was about to release its new robotic dog in 2001, company executives regularly visited chat rooms and bulletin boards. Officially, they offered product news and answered questions. But the fact remains that adults with an ulterior motive went online to find and talk to children.[13]

Beware of Spokes-Puppy

Now that about 90 percent of children's product requests are by brand name, companies strive to be the brand on their lips. As a testament to the influence of young children, Ford Motor Company's Windstar minivan has formed an integrated marketing strategy with Nickelodeon's cartoon series *Blue's Clues*. Ford buys ad time on Nickelodeon and CBS, which runs Nick Jr. on Saturday mornings, and ad space in *Nickelodeon* magazine. Ford uses the animated canine, Blue, as "official spokes-puppy" for its child-safety campaign and sponsors a Blue's Clues tour.[14]

Ford knows what it's doing. By linking the vehicle to a popular children's cartoon character, they are working both angles. As mentioned in Chapter 3, kids have enormous influence over what Mom and Dad buy—direct and indirect influence. Ford also wants to be the preferred brand of these kids when they start buying vehicles, even if they are 12 years shy of driving age.

Crossing the Line

Consumer product companies are fierce competitors and will do just about anything to capture sales. In 1997, the U.S. Federal Trade Commission found Toys 'R' Us, the world's largest toy retailer, guilty of illegally pressuring manufacturers not to supply popular toys to other chains. This ploy reduced options for consumers and foiled their ability to comparison shop.

Yes, consumer product companies go too far with their marketing, and the effect on children can be bizarre. To hype the new Air Jordan XVII, Nike spent $10 million on an ad campaign with TV spots by filmmaker Spike Lee. Packed in a metallic silver briefcase instead of a shoebox, the shoes debuted in February 2002 with a retail price of $200. These are nothing more than fancy sneakers, but Nike succeeded in giving them a sacred aura.

"Most of them will never see the street," said John Shanely of Wells Fargo Securities. "Kids call it a 'keeper.' They basically keep it under their bed and, when friends come over, show it to them."[15]

World's Leading Children's Product Companies Ranked by Sales in 2000 for Ages 5 to 14

Company	Sector
1. Disney	Media, entertainment, theme parks
2. Toys 'R' Us	Retail—toys and games
3. McDonald's	Quick service restaurants
4. Mattel	Toys and games
5. Nestlé	Food and confections
6. Tricon	Quick service restaurants (Taco Bell, KFC, Pizza Hut)
7. Coca-Cola	Beverages
8. Nintendo	Toys and games
9. Pepsico	Food and beverages
10. Hasbro	Toys and games

Source: Euromonitor International Marketing to Children: A World Survey.

Media Conglomerates

Media giants AOL-Time Warner, Viacom, and the Walt Disney Company possess staggering ability to influence behavior, especially in young people. They each command a powerhouse of integrated communication and entertainment across all platforms—television, radio, music, Internet, film, publishing, handheld wireless devices, computer, and phone. They control the channels for reaching and communicating with young people.

A diversified portfolio gives media conglomerates the power to cross-market and cross-sell its young audience at every possible juncture. Advertisers look for as many opportunities as possible to reach children. "It's not just a TV buy anymore but more an overarching relationship with kids and the convergence between programming and promotion opportunities—on-air and off-air, online and off-line," says Joe Uva, president of Turner Entertainment group sales and marketing and part of Time Warner.[16]

It's no coincidence that Disney, the company with the world's largest sales of products and services for children age 5 to 14, also claims the strongest media position in children's marketing and the leading position in the Internet for children. Viacom also has powerful kid connections, especially in television with two networks and a stable of prominent cable channels that include MTV and Nickelodeon.

In 2001, Procter & Gamble took advantage of Viacom's breadth. In a "cross-platform marketing partnership," P&G promoted its brands on 12 Viacom television properties in the United States. The deal helps P&G target the right audience—kids vs. preteens vs. teens vs. young adults, male vs. female, and other demographics—for a particular brand. It also opens the door for co-marketing opportunities, which could include product placements on TV shows, endorsements by TV personalities, or sponsorship of TV events.[17]

The Big Three

AOL TIME WARNER (PRIMARY HOLDINGS)

- TV network: WB
- Cable channels: CNN, HBO, TBS, TNT, Comedy Central (50%), Cinemax, Cartoon Network, Turner Classic Movies, Court TV
- Cable systems: Time Warner Cable
- Magazines: *People, Teen People, Sports Illustrated, Money, In Style, Ski, Entertainment Weekly, Time, Ski, Fortune*
- Music: Atlantic Records, Elektra Entertainment, Warner Bros., Columbia House, Rhino Records, Time Life Music
- Internet: AOL, Netscape, CompuServe, MapQuest, Digital City
- Film studios: Warner Bros., Castle Rock, New Line Cinema, Fine Line Features

VIACOM (PRIMARY HOLDINGS)

- TV networks: CBS and UPN
- Cable channels: MTV, BET, Nickelodeon, Nick at Nite, TV Land, CMT, TNN, VH1, Comedy Central (50%), Showtime, The Movie Channel
- 180+ radio stations
- Blockbuster Video stores
- Publishers: Simon & Schuster, Touchstone, Scribner, Pocket Books, The Free Press, MTV Books, Nickelodeon Books
- Web sites: MTVi Group, Nickelodeon, BET, CBS

The Big Three *(Continued)*

VIACOM *(Continued)*

- Other properties include theme parks, music publishing, outdoor advertising, Star Trek franchise
- Film studios: Paramount Pictures, MTV Films, Nickelodeon Movies

WALT DISNEY COMPANY (PRIMARY HOLDINGS)

- TV network: ABC
- Cable channels: ESPN, A&E, E!, Lifetime, The Disney Channel, SoapNet, The History Channel
- Publishers: Hyperion, Disney, Talk/Miramax Books
- Web sites: ABC, NFL, NBA, NASCAR, Oscar, Disney, Family.com
- Radio syndicate: Disney Radio
- Film studios: Disney, Touchstone, Miramax, Caravan, Hollywood Pictures
- Theme parks
- Other properties include sports teams, daily newspapers, television stations, magazines

Source: PBS *Frontline*: "The Merchants of Cool."

Growing Up with Viacom

Viacom's mix of television properties makes it possible for a child to grow up with Viacom, starting young at Nickelodeon and eventually moving to MTV as a teen. "Nobody says, 'We're going to go after newborns,'" says Pam Kaufman, senior vice president of marketing at Nickelodeon.

"But if you don't get this audience now, you're going to lose them in 10 years."[18]

MTV has been a phenomenal success for Viacom. According to *BusinessWeek*, revenues at MTV International reached $600 million in 2001 and are projected to more than double by 2004.[19] Advertisers crave time on MTV because the format—music videos, live performances, celebrity watching, so-called reality programming, and hosting of decadent parties—mesmerizes teens and young adults. MTV gives kids what they want, and it gives advertisers what they want—a large audience of young consumers.

"The MTV machine doesn't listen to the young so that it can make the young happier. It doesn't listen to the young so it can come up with startling new kinds of music. The MTV machine tunes in so that it can figure out how to pitch what Viacom has to sell to those kids," said Mark Crispin Miller, NYU professor of media ecology, media critic, and author.[20]

Behind Closed Doors

Like most media conglomerates, Viacom and MTV pour huge amounts of money into research so they can develop programming that attracts an audience that advertisers want to reach. However, MTV takes research to a creepy level.

"Ever since the very beginning, there's been a kind of feverish addiction to research and understanding young people," said Todd Cunningham, senior vice president of Strategy and Planning for MTV, which conducts more than 200 focus groups a year.[21] MTV also goes one-on-one to pick kids' brains in an annual ethnography study, which attempts to understand subtle differences that separate segments of an audience. Researchers literally rifle through their closets, check out their music collections, go to nightclubs with them, and get very personal.

"We shut the door in their bedrooms and talk to them about issues that they feel are really important to them," Cunningham said in an interview with PBS. "We talk with them about what it's like to date today; what it's like dealing with their parents; what things stress them out the most; what things are really on the hearts and minds of them and their peers. We have them show us their favorite clothing outfits, what they wear to parties, some things from their photo albums and things that really mean something to them. And then we're allowed to come back and translate that into programming opportunities or just insights in general about what the audience actually does."[22]

MTV does this all in the name of understanding what makes young viewers tick and, more specifically, understanding their wants. "What this system does is it closely studies the young, keeps them under constant surveillance to figure out what will push their buttons," says media critic Mark Crispin Miller. "And it blares it back at them relentlessly and everywhere."[23]

Much like consumer product companies, media companies show no regard for the welfare of children when there's a buck to be made. An FTC report in September 2000 concluded that movie, music, and video game industries aggressively market adult-rated wares to underage children. The FTC found that 80 percent of R-rated movies, 70 percent of "mature" video games, and all 55 music recordings with labels for "explicit" content were marketed to children under 17.[24]

"They knew what they were doing," said FTC chairman Robert Pitofsky. The agency claimed that company executives were aware that youngsters would see TV commercials and movie theater trailers that feature shooting, expletives, sexuality, and references to rape and mutilation. Some PG-13 movies with licensed action toys had advertised during Saturday morning cartoons that appeal to young children.[25]

Advertising Agencies

At the 2002 Talking to Teens Conference, attendees from companies across the United States and Canada came with one shared objective: learn how to sell more stuff to kids. One of several similar conferences, it offered to teach participants the art of marketing to youngsters.

Speaker after speaker told how to launch an assault on the lucrative teen market. A session called "The Teen Hunter" was presented by self-proclaimed "teen marketing guru" Craig Yoe, former creative director for Jim Henson's Muppets. Nicole Witt, marketing manager at Eastman Kodak, explained how her team developed an advertising campaign and marketing program that increased brand usage and loyalty among teens by playing off the three teen conflicts: autonomy vs. belonging; idealism vs. pragmatism; and narcissism vs. intimacy. Procter & Gamble described social network marketing. AT&T Wireless defined exoloopaphobia.

The conference was loaded with incredibly creative thinkers. Session after session provided ideas on how to leverage and exploit teens in their many different environments. The ethical or moral implications of their manipulative plans were never mentioned.

Fresh off the conference, I presented a workshop and decided to share those details with a room full of parents. When told about the different sessions and the objective of the conference, the general consensus was disgust and disbelief.

A New Specialty

Youth marketing has evolved to the point where large agencies have separate divisions devoted to child-focused products, smaller agencies specialize in youth advertising or youth research, and conferences share the secrets of making kids want what you're selling. Newsletters like *Youth Markets Alert* provide details on the latest high-profile marketing campaigns, demographic trends, and marketing research. The Golden Marble Awards, sponsored by *KidScreen*, a trade magazine for "those involved in reaching children through entertainment," honor the best in advertising for children.

An editorial in *The Boston Globe* objected to the Golden Marble Awards, noting that "advertising executives are brazenly patting themselves on the back for getting children hooked onto junk food and video games. . . . Many winners of the last two years add up to a chamber of horrors in a nation facing an epidemic of child obesity: Hostess pastries, Oreo cookies, Pepsi, McDonald's, Burger King, Post and Kellogg's cereals, and Nintendo."[26]

Ad agencies, plus their colleagues in research, marketing and public relations firms, are in business to produce results for consumer product companies. They pull no punches in their efforts to understand what works and what doesn't and to create advertising, promotions, and other communications that click with consumers, even if they're children. That kind of mentality inspired Joe Camel.

Probing the Youth Network

Look-Look, one of the leading research agencies in the youth market, offers an online, real-time research and information service focused on global youth culture. The agency has recruited a network of more than 10,000 young people who report on the lives of 14- to 30-year-olds.[27]

These trendsetters, selected to represent the 20 percent of the youth population who influence the other 80 percent, offer insights into young people's changing attitudes on fashion, entertainment, technology, health and beauty, food, and more. With a click of a mouse, Look-Look clients can query select segments of the youth network with an instant poll. And that's what they promise their consumer product company clients—instant feedback. In a market that is known for fickle-minded consumers, the efforts of Look-Look move one step closer to being inside the head of every youth segment imaginable.[28]

What Advertising?

Working to overcome suspicion or distrust among consumers, agencies increasingly look for subtle ways to promote a product without using direct advertising. In 2001, Child's Play Communications helped Larami, a division of Hasbro, introduce a bigger, more powerful line of Super Soaker squirt guns designed for teens. In addition to placing articles in publications and on teen web sites, the agency recruited radio stations in major markets for promotions on the air and demonstrations at special events. The agency sent free Super Soakers to music groups like Green Day to use in their stage performances, which were shown on MTV. Child's Play also worked with product placement specialists and TV production companies to place Super Soakers on television shows that appeal to teens.[29]

The same agency recently announced a new service that helps clients get products and information into the hands of kids and the moms who buy for them. "The new Child's Play 'Kid Contact' team will hit the streets of your chosen markets, distributing product samples and information to your target audience where they 'live' from soccer fields and baseball stadiums to movie lines, music concerts and malls," the agency said. Child's Play also offers to help reach kids in schools—preschools on up—and to promote clients' products on youth-targeted Internet sites.[30]

Pushing Buttons

Once they have gathered enough information through research, agencies try to pinpoint how to get kids to make the desired response. Often aided by child psychologists, agencies figure out how to push the buttons on a child's insecurities and other weaknesses.

"Advertising at its best is making people feel that without your product, they're a loser. Kids are very sensitive to that," said Nancy Shalek, of the Grey Advertising Agency. "If you tell them to buy something, they're resistant. But if you tell them that they'll be a dork if they don't, you've got their attention. You open up emotional vulnerabilities and it's very easy to do this with kids because they're the most emotionally vulnerable."[31]

Allen Kanner, Ph.D., a clinical psychologist at the Wright Institute in Berkeley, California, understands Shalek's perspective and doesn't approve: "Advertising is a massive, multibillion dollar project that's having an enormous impact on child development. Thanks to advertising, children have become convinced that they are inferior if they don't have an endless array of new products."[32]

Kanner said research conducted at the university level frequently guides pitches to children. "They are taking this very sophisticated understanding of children's relationships and what they respond to, and then really tailoring it to the advertisement and refining it," he said.[33] For example, psychologist and kid marketing expert Dan Acuff details how to pull the strings of kids in his book, *What Kids Buy and Why: The Psychology of Marketing to Kids*. To get better results for advertisers, Acuff and his partner, Dr. Robert Reiher, invented the Youth Market System, which derived from extensive research on children's cognitive development. Their clients include Nike, Microsoft, Disney, Pepsi, Hasbro, Warner Brothers, Mattel, Coca-Cola, ABC, and CBS.[34]

In Defense of Children

In September 1999, a letter signed by 60 prominent psychologists and sent to the president of the American Psychological Association condemned using insights and research methods of psychology to sell products to children. The letter said these practices are epidemic and are done with the complicity of psychologists.[35] "The result is an enormous advertising and marketing onslaught that comprises, arguably, the largest single psychological project ever undertaken," the letter stated. In addition, the letter claimed that members of the association violated the group's mission by using their knowledge "to promote and assist the commercial exploitation and manipulation of children."[36]

Timothy Kasser, associate professor of psychology at Knox College, Galesburg, Illinois, was among those who signed the letter. "When advertisers are using psychological principles to sell products to children, they are not only selling the product, but they are also selling a larger value system that says making money and using your money for the purchase of material things will make you happy," he said. "That's what is really behind almost every commercial message, that this product will make you feel happy or loved or safe and secure. My feeling is that it is manipulation to use children's needs to get them to buy these products."[37]

The letter urged the APA to:

- Denounce the use of psychological techniques to assist corporate marketing and advertising to children.
- Amend the APA's Ethics Code to establish limits for psychologists on the use of psychological knowledge or techniques to observe, study, manipulate, harm, exploit, mislead, trick, or deceive children for commercial purpose.

- Probe, review, and confront the use of psychological research in advertising and marketing to children.[38]

What a Child Believes

Advertisers and agencies defend their actions, saying that kids are more savvy than ever before and have the ability to weigh advertising claims. Katie Milligan, of the Center for a New American Dream, disagrees: "Young children simply do not possess the skills to screen commercials for the accuracy and truthfulness of their promises and thus are vulnerable to suggestive imagery and misleading (often implicit) claims in ads. Study after study has confirmed that most young children have trouble distinguishing when TV programs end and the commercials begin. The majority of young kids do not even understand the purpose of a commercial is to sell something."[39]

She contends that advertising exploits a child's naivete. After viewing a commercial for Cocoa Pebbles cereal featuring Fred Flintstone and Barney Rubble, one study found that four- to seven-year-olds wanted the cereal in part because it would make them smile and because Fred and Barney recommended it. One-third of the children believed the cartoon characters were nutritional experts.[40]

A Time for Outrage

The Boston Globe painted a bleak picture when it noted "how deep our children stand in commercialism's grand canyon. Turn to the west and they are staring at Hollywood's soaring walls of media violence. Turn to the east and there is the sheer face of Madison Avenue's cold-blooded manipulation of children's minds."[41] Unfortunately, there seems to be no limit to the depths of this canyon. A recent item in *KidScreen*, the youth ad magazine, suggests parents have more to fear: "Agencies are cautiously eyeing the zero-to-three (years old) demographic, a group that poses tremendous challenges and opportunities because research has indicated that children are capable of understanding brands at very young ages."[42]

Pete Blackshaw, a former brand manager for Procter & Gamble, says marketers, including P&G, are at a critical crossroads. "There is a lack of discipline in the marketing system now. It's not consumer-centric, and that will backfire on all of us," says Blackshaw. "The companies that win in the next decade will be 200 percent candid in their marketing and will need to draw lines where ads are or are not welcome and acceptable."[43]

Jeff Goodby, of ad agency Goodby, Silverstein & Partners in San Francisco, says he's surprised at the level of commercialism in sports and education so far. "The vines have already grown around the house," he says. "I thought the public would have rebelled by now. Instead, people say they don't like sports commercialism and then they put on their Nike shirt and go to the game."[44]

Just a few short years ago, society was outraged to learn tobacco companies and their ad agencies had targeted children with manipulative marketing. Isn't it curious how few parents notice that their kids are being manipulated by hundreds of other consumer product companies? Never before in our nation's history has an entire generation been peddled to with such energy and sophistication. Marketers spend billions of dollars shaping the opinions of young people, nurturing their consumer appetites, and reinforcing their spend-happy patterns and habits.

The collective force of this drive is virtually beyond comprehension. But parents need to recognize this crisis, this assault, for the sake of their children. Unless you challenge marketing efforts, you surrender influence and power to promoters of the Teen Commandments.

Money Talks

- How does marketing and advertising targeted to young people compare between now and when you were your child's age?
- How do you feel about the marketing tactics described in this chapter?
- How you feel about companies that use these tactics?
- What do you think about the use of child psychology in advertising?
- Does the three-headed monster play fair in its chess game with children?

Chapter SIX

Where's the Rest of the Village?

Apopular African proverb suggests it takes a village to raise a child. Hillary Rodham Clinton said she chose that proverb as a book title "because it offers a timeless reminder that children will only thrive if their families thrive and if the whole of society cares enough to provide for them."[1] However, the consumer culture has radically distorted this concept. In the United States, children fail to thrive financially because the whole of society apparently doesn't care enough to provide for them. Rodham Clinton writes that, in addition to other social ills, children are under siege "from greed, materialism and spiritual emptiness."[2]

Are we so caught up in having more that we are blind to the consequences? And what about the companies that hunt down young people in pursuit of the almighty dollar. Do they have any ethical or moral responsibility for their openly manipulative actions?

Due to lack of awareness and accountability, willingness to compromise values, political cowardice, and cold-blooded profit motive, the village looks away rather than act to protect your children and their financial future. As the consumer culture advances, culprits can be found throughout the village, including places you'd least suspect.

Exploited by Business

In the previous chapter, I called out the conniving and cunning tactics that are standard operating procedure for the three-headed monster. But why is this happening? What is the motive for companies to abandon any ethical discussion of right and wrong when peddling products to young people? Could part of it be overly ambitious profit expectations? It's as if they will do whatever it takes to increase shareholder value.

Recently, leading corporations in the United States have crashed and burned by taking incredible business risk. As such, it would appear that corporations' obsession and pressure to demonstrate short-term earnings success supersedes any dialogue on the potential negative impact of their exploitive practices. At least in some industries there are standards that must be maintained to stay in business. Consider the rigid guidelines of the Environmental Protection Agency.

And what about the responsibility of a company's board of directors? Why aren't they asking more questions and advocating for the consumer? Because many of them are either in the dark or passive bystanders as companies concoct schemes that addict kids to spending.

And where are the industry standards? Are there any lines the three-headed monster won't cross trying to brand their products with the massive youth audience? Once again, it proves that companies have totally abandoned any ethical conversations of how their methods impact the consumer. I am sure the response "That's not our problem" has been repeated ad nauseam. But remember, the tobacco industry paid dearly for crossing the line of acceptability.

How ironic that this short-sighted, self-serving approach might compromise the United States' financial future. What happens if these bright, young people wake up and realize that they have been manipulated? Imagine the economic impact if they decided to express their displeasure by boycotting the brands that target youth.

Remember, protesting is in their genes. Certainly, we haven't forgotten how their parents reshaped the political landscape in the late '60s and early '70s. Could today's young people be destined to reshape the consumer landscape?

Sold Out by Schools

I give American schools two F's. One for failing to teach basic consumer finance. The other for failing to protect children from predatory marketers.

Outside of the guidance provided in the home, teachers may have the greatest impact in shaping the lives of kids. Each school day, millions of families entrust the future of their children to public and private educational systems. How are schools doing with this enormous responsibility? There are two key indicators: financial literacy and in-school marketing. For many, these issues aren't even on their radar screen. For the observant, these two threats may be keeping you up at night.

F in Teaching Financial Literacy

As mentioned in Chapter 2, the financial literacy of our nation's young people is bad and getting worse. Let me quickly recap: In a 1997 survey, high school seniors answered correctly only 57 percent of questions on income, money management, saving and investing, and spending and credit. In 2002, scores fell even lower, to just 50 percent of questions answered correctly.[3]

When I asked a parent to comment on the results, he said, "They're young. Give them time out in the real world." That's not a good idea, though. Nearly 50 percent of adults failed a similar test![4]

According to the National Council on Economic Education, 38 states have adopted standards or guidelines for teaching economics, but only 13 states actually require students to take an economics course. "Some people feel that money matters, like sex, should be discussed at home, not at school," said NCEE President Robert Duvall.[5] But if 49 percent of the adults are failing, what, if anything, is being taught at home?

Children need to learn basic consumer and financial principles—everything from budgeting to comparison shopping to understanding compound interest. But schools generally don't teach financial skills—skills that have life-long value.

F at In-School Marketing

Parents entrust schools to take care of their children. They rightfully assume there's no safer place than an elementary schoolroom under the watchful eye of a teacher. Guess again. The fact is that many schools let strangers talk to your kids. Advertisers reach children through mandatory viewing of commercials, sponsored textbooks, exclusive soft drink contracts, and even in-school market research.

The plot thickens. School districts facing budget pressure frantically look for alternative revenue sources. Enter the highly controversial Channel One. For over ten years, the media company has persuaded over 12,000 schools with some eight million students to air its 12-minute daily current events program. Participating schools receive $25,000 worth of video equipment. The catch: The programming is ten minutes of news and two minutes of commercials for youth-oriented products, like Mountain Dew, Nike, and Snickers.[6] Each 30-second spot sells for approximately $200,000 which, in 1999, meant $346 million in ad revenues for Channel One.[7] During one school year, Channel One viewing adds up to one solid week of school time, or about one full day of watching commercials.

Channel One can charge premium rates because it offers advertisers a captive audience. In exchange for the electronic gear, schools promise that students will watch. When Channel One flashes on the screen, schools require children to give their undivided attention to the news program and the commercials.

If you think the folks at Channel One have a real interest in educational programming, think again. At a 1994 youth marketing conference, the then-president of Channel One stated its true value: "The biggest selling point to advertisers [is that] . . . we are forcing kids to watch two minutes of commercials. . . . The advertiser gets a group of kids who cannot go to the bathroom, who cannot change the station, who cannot listen to their mother yell in the background, who cannot be playing Nintendo, who cannot have their headsets on."[8]

Channel One has paved the way for even more stealth marketing organizations. In its report "Cashing in on Kids," the Center for the Analysis of Commercialism in Education said commercial activities in schools have risen more than 300 percent since 1990.[9] Educational marketing agencies specialize in creating, producing, and distributing corporate-sponsored curriculum to schools, a market that includes over 60 million children, 80 million parents, and 3 million teachers.[10]

At the Talking to Teens conference I attended, Don Lay, managing director of Learning Works, an educational marketing and advertising firm, presented a seminar on in-school marketing. "Teachers will do almost anything for us because of the state of the educational system," he said. "The biggest problem teachers have, day in and day out, is a lack of time to plan, so we create high-quality, classroom-ready educational materials that match the day-to-day needs of the teachers with the marketing objectives of our clients."[11]

Learning Works offers a wide range of "educational" materials, such as activity books, bilingual programs, book covers, computer software, newsletters, study guides, teacher training programs, and more. All are sponsored by Learning Works clients, such as AT&T, The Gillette Company, McDonald's, Universal Pictures, Ford Motor Company, Snack Food Association, Hasbro Toys, ABC, NBC, CBS, Lee Jeans, Max Factor, and MCI WorldCom.[12] Over the last several years, corporations have grown more aggressive. "What used to be warm and fuzzy, altruistic programs for schools are now immediate-sales and long-term brand driven," Lay said.[13]

Staffed mainly by former teachers, Learning Works promises to "reach only those schools, teachers and families that you want to reach." The agency targets specific TV viewing areas; select schools based on their size, ethnic composition, or median household income; or schools that have fully integrated technology into their curriculum.[14]

Using its up-to-date database, the agency typically contacts teachers directly. "We avoid getting permission from the school district because the red tape is enormous," Lay said.[15] Of the teachers they contacted, 86 percent integrated the materials into the classroom and 63 percent hand out company literature and product samples, Lay said.[16]

The masters of lucrative product placement deals inside schools are Coke and Pepsi. Across the country, thousands of school districts have sold the exclusive marketing rights in exchange for big cash payments. In fact, some schools have negotiated long-term deals that net the district several million dollars a year. The proceeds help finance everything from school landscaping to uniforms for school workers, and scoreboards.

It sounds easy and harmless. Consider the ten-year exclusive contract between Coke and the Colorado Springs school district. The contract stated they had to sell at least 70,000 cases of Coke products during one of the first three years, otherwise payments would be significantly reduced in the remaining seven years.[17] In a letter written to school principals, district executive John Bushey wrote that not enough soda and other Coke products were being sold to earn the big dollars promised in the contract. He encouraged principals to make sure the vending machines were easily accessible to students.[18]

Where is the student voice? Colorado Springs is just one example where districts have compromised the health and well-being of the students to make up for the financial shortfall that appears to be getting worse, not better. Unfortunately, the slippery slope is in place. Today soda companies, tomorrow . . .

More F's for Our Village

F in Integrity

Colleges and universities also earn a failing grade for selling out students. They sell access to students to the most aggressive marketers of all, the credit card companies. Once again, the very institutions that parents trust as *de facto* guardians open the door for lions to feast on lambs.

According to Robert Manning, author of *Credit Card Nation*, credit card companies direct their marketing efforts at the 250 largest public schools and their highly profitable student populations.[19] For example, in a seven-year, $16.5 million deal, the University of Tennessee gives First USA access to student names, addresses, and phone numbers. The university also receives annual royalty fees of $1 per new account, $3 on the one-year anniversary of each existing account, and up to 0.5 percent of net retail sales charged to each account.[20]

A trip to most college and university campuses shows the credit card companies in action. On some campuses, like the University of Tennessee, they have booths giving away T-shirts, electronic equipment, and other free stuff in exchange for a signature on the application. While smaller schools may not have the big buck contracts, "moles" put up posters in classroom buildings and dormitories to seduce students with the latest low-rate card. "Even though credit card solicitations are banned from campus, we know some companies pay students to keep their literature visible," said Keith, a vice president at a small liberal arts college in Iowa.

One young student at the University of Wisconsin described a phone call he received in his dorm room within his first month on campus: "The phone rings and it's a hard sales pitch for a credit card. I decline the offer and don't think much of it until I hear the phone ring in the room next door. Same hard sales pitch. And for the next several minutes, you could hear the phone ringing one room right after another down the hallway for the same high pressure offer."

Credit card companies also lure young adults with advertising that pushes the independence button and the forget-reality button. Two ads appearing on college campuses illustrate the temptation of credit cards:

> "Free from parental rule at last. Now all you need is money. **CHA-CHING!** Get 3% cash back on everything you buy"—Visa.[21]

> "Money Can't Buy You Love, But A Credit Card Can Get You Started"—MasterCard/Visa.[22]

Credit card companies are desperate for exposure on college and university campuses for two primary reasons.

First, the average person keeps his or her first credit card for approximately 15 years, so getting into a student's wallet first can be a bonanza for the credit card company.[23] With interest rates and late fees, there are millions to be made on the backs of debt-laden students. Second, if a student gets in over his head, the "automatic bailout system" kicks in. Credit card companies know that Mom and Dad usually come to the rescue. I saw this firsthand when I presented the workshop, "Your Money, Your Future: Take Control," to more than 2000 students at eight colleges during the fall of 2001.

Mark, a high school senior, told me about his plans to go to college next fall. Most teens are thrilled to talk about their big decision. In Mark's case, his energy sagged as he described how the entire college fund his parents had saved went to pay off the consumer debts of his older brother, who had just graduated. Mark shrugged it off, but the look on his face told otherwise. Paying for college was now his responsibility.

F in Financial Training

Despite their reputation as a training ground for life in the "real world," colleges and universities rarely talk to students about important financial realities. Virtually no college or university offers consumer-based financial education. However, a growing handful have discovered a need to provide debt counseling services.

Schools like the University of Minnesota find that excess consumer debt affects students' ability to stay enrolled, which ultimately affects their ability to repay student loans.

Tom, a certified credit counselor who works with college students in Minnesota, agreed that colleges do little to teach financial skills. "The only time I see the school interested in talking to students about money is just before they graduate, when they are required to meet with a university-sponsored financial counselor," he said. The purpose of that meeting: establish a plan for paying back your student loans.

Higher education has taken the low road. Colleges and universities are more interested in getting their money back than in helping students prepare for financial life. They are more interested in brokering students for credit card companies than in teaching students how to manage or avoid debt.

I wonder if these same schools think about the impact this could have on future donations. After all, if your fond memories of college include several thousand dollars of high-interest credit card debt, you probably won't run for your checkbook to participate in the next alumni donor drive.

Abandoned by Government

The federal government is either asleep at the switch or conveniently looking the other way—or both—when it comes to the multibillion-dollar industry of marketing to kids.

Open Season on Kids

The U.S. Congress sided with business and against children in 1980 when it passed Public Law 96-252.[24] This law *prohibits* the Federal Trade Commission (FTC) from enacting any rules in children's advertising. As a result, the key regulatory agency in this field has no ability to protect kids from being targeted for manipulative advertising messages. Is this how Congress protects kids? They could just as well have declared open season on children for marketing predators.

In 1997, FTC Commissioner Roscoe B. Starek III said that protecting children from unfair and deceptive practices

99

remains a priority for the Federal Trade Commission. However, he also made it clear that the FTC maintains a hands-off policy on advertising to children.[25]

"Self-regulation and consumer education can go a long way toward accomplishing this goal," he said, "and I can predict that the Commission will continue to encourage private efforts to empower parents and protect children. We cannot and should not dictate the form of self-regulation, however, or attempt to regulate by threat of Commission action in areas where we lack authority. To do so needlessly risks stifling the burgeoning innovative efforts of the private sector."[26]

Other countries have acted to protect their children. After reviewing research on children's ability to understand advertising, the government in Sweden banned all commercial TV ads directed at kids under the age of 12. Norway prohibits advertising toys on television to children between 7 A.M. and 10 P.M. Quebec prohibits TV ads directed at children below the age of 13.[27]

But there are no restrictions in the United States. Remember, this is the same government that created the world's most complicated tax code and insists on years of testing before releasing a new pharmaceutical as a way to protect the health of U.S. citizens. This is the same government that set the national drinking age at 21 and supports "drug-free zones" around thousands of primary and secondary schools.

In an open letter to the Surgeon General, Dr. Richard H. Carmona, hundreds of child advocates addressed a variety of child health issues, including in-school advertising. "Parents and children across the country need their Surgeon General to be courageous enough to promote children's health, even if it conflicts with the interests of industries with considerable political power," wrote Gary Ruskin, executive director of Commercial Alert.[28]

Payback Time

Should we ignore the nearly 150,000 young people under age 25 who will file bankruptcy this year and the hundreds of thousands more who may soon fall into the financial abyss?

Ironically, Congress is on the verge of enacting new legislation that would make it more difficult to file personal bankruptcy. Credit card providers have eased their standards and extended credit lines to people who would have been rejected in years past. The credit card companies accepted that risk. Now they want more protection and exert enormous lobbying pressure to make it more difficult for individuals to escape their Mt. Everest of consumer debt.

Don't expect the White House to look out for the little guy. MBNA, the credit card behemoth, was one of the largest contributors to the Bush presidential campaign at just over $3 million.[29] Democrats and Republicans have accepted millions from credit card companies to protect their interests. How disappointing that neither Congress nor the White House will do the right thing and clamp down on predatory, manipulative, and deceptive practices in youth marketing. A government of the people, for the people, and by the people rings hollow.

Government put its head in the sand on the welfare of young people, and no change appears likely anytime soon. Companies have the government's permission to stalk your child in schools and on the Internet, to seduce your child into buying stuff he or she doesn't need, to brainwash your child into thinking the American way means buying whatever you want and embracing credit card debt. Alan Greenspan, the Federal Reserve Chairman, has repeatedly asked Congress to consider the impact financially illiterate children will have on our future economy. He worries about their long-term financial health, yet he offers no challenge to the three-headed monster for more ethical and responsible behavior.

To the logical person, Congress and others in federal government appear willing to trade America's children for short-term corporate profits, which is just a marketer's phrase for greed. Can somebody say campaign finance reform?

Overlooked by Religion

Robert Wuthnow, a Princeton University sociologist, argues that materialism is a social problem. "It is built into the fabric of society itself, pressuring us to conform to it, shaping our lives by virtue of the sheer fact that we cannot escape living in a society any more than we can escape eating and sleeping."[30]

Of all the areas in the village where young people could learn to shape their financial philosophy, especially in the area of sharing, religious institutions may have the greatest upside potential. Consider the unique opportunities to interface with people of all backgrounds, differing in socioeconomic level, race, gender, and age. Frequent gatherings of these groups are ripe for initiating dialogue on critical topics for healthy living and prosperous relationships. That's the good news.

The bad news is that religious organizations have abdicated their role of helping young people shape their financial values. Isn't it ironic? Businesses can't spend money fast enough shaping children's financial habits, and religious organizations don't give them the time of day.

Unfortunately, most churches don't teach or guide young people in their financial journey. In its book, *Growing Up Generous*, the Alban Institute detailed how it came up empty in searching for religious organizations that are models for teaching young people about sharing money. "After contacting more than 100 Christian churches nationwide, we found no church that was assertively or innovatively encouraging youth to give financially," the authors wrote.[31]

Many in the religious community have children, watch TV, and understand the push to spend early and spend often. But they don't teach young people lessons on appropriate spending, on saving, or even on how to share their money.

The Alban Institute report lists seven obstacles that religious organizations face in teaching youth about money and giving:

1. **Discomfort with talking about money.** "Today we talk about sex, we talk about religion in many different kinds of ways, and we talk about politics . . . but we still don't talk about money," said Dwight Burlingame of Indiana University's Center on Philanthropy.[32]

   The difficulty comes in crossing over from the secular to the sacred. Robert Wuthnow writes in his book, *God and Mammon in America:* "(I)n our own society, most of us have been taught to think of money in purely secular terms. Reading *Money* magazine, paging through *The Wall Street Journal,* or taking a course in economics, we gain the impression that money is simply a medium of exchange. . . . If we think about our own views of money, though, we know that it is much more than economists lead us to believe. It has meaning. And it is thus connected with our beliefs and values—whether we admit it or not."[33]

2. **Loss of tradition to motivate giving.**[34] When many of our parents and grandparents were growing up, there was an understanding that you gave first to your place of worship. Giving was part of their culture, taking priority over other consumer activities. Over the last few

decades, the traditions faded as overwhelming marketing and consumer pressure moved us farther from gratitude and closer to greed. "There is a kind of mental or emotional gloss to contemporary religious teachings about money that prevents them from having much impact on how people actually live their lives," Wuthnow writes.[35] As young people struggle to align their faith with their financial values, the church fails to infuse lasting commitment to sharing their time, talents, and treasures.

3. **Competing and confusing messages.**[36] When I was growing up, even young people received offering envelopes as a way to acknowledge their importance in the giving process. However, for most congregations, budget cuts did away with that simple ritual. Unfortunately, there is powerful truth to "out of sight, out of mind."

   The authors of *Growing Up Generous* contend there are more questions than answers on youth and giving: Why should young people give?[37] To what or whom should young people give? Excellent questions, but few in the church give them much consideration.

4. **An exclusive focus on institutional needs.**[38] The struggle between immediate and deferred gratification visits more and more churches. In times of financial hardships, the temptation to focus energy and dialogue on the church's immediate needs steals attention from the long-term financial journey of the individual. Some would say the practice of overemphasizing institutional needs is nothing new. However, the compounding effect of neglect may last for generations.

5. **Lack of emphasis, guidance or teaching.**[39] The focus on institutional needs overshadows important questions about money, materialism, and giving from a faith perspective.

The reason I was approached in 1990 by Sally, the religious educator, to write *Parents, Kids & Money* was that the church offered surprisingly little on this topic. She observed and was concerned about kids' lopsided consumer perspective on money issues. Sally felt a strong need to bring young people and their parents together so they could explore the role money plays in their lives.

As word spread, more and more churches began asking about the resource. Soon after, I was approached to write *Parents, Teens & Money*.

6. **Financial anxieties of clergy and youth leaders.**[40] I personally have observed many clergy and youth workers who lack a well-developed financial vocabulary and feel uncomfortable engaging young people in financial conversations. One significant problem is that clergy receive little financial training in seminary. The parallel would be a corporate leader who has no formal training in managing a budget or no understanding of the capital required to maintain a physical plant.

Another contributing factor is that many clergy and youth workers have amassed significant debt in completing their education and struggle to meet routine financial obligations. One former youth pastor in Pennsylvania confided that he left the ministry because he couldn't pay his monthly bills. Even though his lifestyle was modest, his salary wasn't enough to cover expenses and student loans. Rather than go through the humiliation of filing bankruptcy, he left for a higher paying job in the for-profit sector.

7. **Belief that youth shouldn't be expected to give.**[41] Plenty of reasons support this reluctance: Youth don't have much money. They might leave if asked to give. They need to save. Their parents already give. The most

105

popular might be that their overall financial contributions are minimal, so why use valuable resources to help them ponder the role money plays in their lives?

Again, the church misses an opportunity to talk with young people about the joy of giving, not the obligation of giving. By failing to engage youth and their parents in conversations on giving, the church fails to offer a counter-rhythm to the flood of messages encouraging kids to spend.

The Church Can Do More

The seven obstacles point to significant shortcomings in the church. For all the energy the three-headed monster allocates to hypnotizing kids with warped consumer values, the church plays a passive bystander, distracted by "more important" matters.

For years, religious institutions have missed critical opportunities to work with young people and their parents as they contemplate their own financial philosophy. Just as the State of Minnesota has done with Target Market, a campaign that empowers kids to take on the tobacco industry, religious organizations could inspire young people to question the social implications of blatant consumer manipulation.[42] As I said earlier, there is no better place to bring together diverse people to learn about and debate world hunger, homelessness, and other issues that challenge our consumer-crazy ways.

Spoiled by Relatives

After a workshop in southern California, a couple with two elementary-age kids approached me. "Help" was the first word out of their mouths. They described how both sets of grandparents were corrupting any semblance of financial balance and values in their kids.

106

Birthdays and other holidays had turned into a competition for who could buy more stuff. Part of the problem they attributed to geographic separation, but they also sensed the grandparents believed that presents would make their grandchildren love them more. As the kids got older, the extravagance worsened. Sucked into the game, the kids played one set of grandparents off the other. In time, the parents had to hide presents to manage their kids' expectations.

Who would have thought that your own family could undermine your efforts to instill fiscal responsibility? Unfortunately, they tell a common story. If I had a dollar for every time a parent shared a story of an overindulgent relative, I could make a significant contribution to my favorite charity.

Today, one-third of all U.S. adults are grandparents. According to *American Demographics* magazine, they spend an average of $500 a year on their grandchildren, almost double the amount spent 10 years earlier. The average age of a first-time grandparent today is 47, giving them an enormous amount of time to indulge their grandchildren.[43]

Parents find themselves in an odd conundrum. How do you deliver the message that the grandparents' generosity is a problem? One woman from Chicago told me she confronted her mother about the pattern of excess. "Mom," she said, "you send boxes upon boxes of gifts each Christmas while we work to encourage simplicity. Please support our position." Her mother was deeply offended, leaving a strain in their relationship.

Or what about the family that lives within minutes of grandparents who offer a treat—a little trinket or toy or special food—*every time* the kids visit. The psychologist Pavlov discovered that ringing a bell before dispensing a treat to a dog eventually trains the dog to salivate profusely when the bell rings. Spot, meet Johnny and Sarah, the grandkids. Grandparents and other relatives need to look in the mirror and ask themselves, "What response are we teaching?"

Many of these people lived through the Depression or grew up in a home where living within your means was gospel. How surprising that they can't control their consumer impulses. It's as if growing up with so little food, clothing, and material possessions somehow justifies the lavish behavior.

Ultimately, the very people most qualified to question the lack of financial values in our society play right into the hands of the three-headed monster. The "greatest generation" could do so much more. They could lead by example, share stories of what it was like to get by with so little, and discourage unnecessary gift giving. My greatest memories of my grandparents aren't linked to some toy they gave me, but rather an experience we shared.

Imagine if, for one year, grandparents took half of the money they spend on grandchildren and instead made a donation to the child's favorite cause. Now that's a lesson to remember.

What's the Answer?

As a parent, you have a right to expect support from the rest of the village. However, be prepared to hear a laundry list of excuses for not doing more. Despite evidence of the consumer culture's corrupting effect on children, the village has been slow to recognize the problem. The time to act is now. For the welfare and financial future of America's children, all parties in the village need to look squarely at the issue and live up to their responsibilities. Let me offer a few suggestions.

To the three-headed monster: We know the temptation is high for you to keep swinging the hypnotic watch of consumerism in the face of young people. However, before implementing your next stealth marketing campaign, ask a group of parents from different socioeconomic backgrounds for their input. Routinely arrange for consumer watchdog groups to run an ethical litmus test for your marketing and advertising plans. Be proactive on ethics and child welfare. Not long ago, the tobacco companies thought they were untouchable. Their lapse of ethics cost them hundreds of billions of dollars.

To schools and colleges: You're likely to continue wrestling with tight budgets and will face increased pressure to compromise the "commercial-free zone." You will be under siege by companies offering to ease your financial pain, if you let them cozy up to your students. Review school policies, hold public forums, and question the future impact before saying yes to "generous" corporate sponsors. Implement plans for improving financial literacy at all levels. The earlier young people have the skills to make informed financial decisions, the more successful they'll be at understanding the role money plays in their lives.

To members of Congress: By addressing this issue, you have more to lose than to gain especially in contributions to your political campaigns. However, once parents become aware of this crisis, their 80 million votes could swing elections at every level. For all the talk about how kids are the future, now's your chance to walk the walk. Become an advocate for children. Start by giving the FTC more authority over predatory marketing practices and passing legislation to require that schools offer a basic financial curriculum. Seek the counsel of the American Psychological Association and carefully consider their recommendation on advertising to children. Do it for the long-term financial health of the country. If you don't, the financial and social fallout of a generation addicted to spending could be staggering.

To the religious community: First, help fill the spiritual vacuum created by excessive consumerism. It's your role and you've abdicated it. Second, when it comes to youth and money, adopt a long-term view. Remember, you reap what you sow. Provide ample educational opportunities. Encourage young people to wrestle with issues of consumerism and the role money plays in their lives. Question whether you have devoted adequate resources at the local, regional, and national level to do the job. Your future depends on people generously sharing their time, talent, and money. By helping young people establish balanced financial values and appropriate financial boundaries, your contributions to society could be enormous.

To grandparents and other relatives: Because of your role in the family, you have a unique opportunity to impact future behavior. Step back and examine your own behavior first. It might be fun and easy to lavish your grandchildren with stuff, but exercising restraint and helping them understand the importance of prudent financial decisions can impact their outlook for decades. Share with them your financial values, particularly how you balance spending, saving, and sharing. Talk about how good it feels to save for a goal or share money with a worthy cause. Give them more than gifts, and you will add a valuable dimension to their lives.

With these suggestions, I hope to begin a long-overdue dialogue on the roles and responsibility of the village in shaping young people's financial values. While every area of the village can contribute, the collective energy of the whole will ultimately determine the outcome. Don't wait for someone else to lead the charge. Your child needs you to start fighting the erosion of financial boundaries today. Ask questions. Advocate change. Expect more from yourself and from others in your village.

Money Talks

- What do you think is Corporate America's responsibility to respect the welfare of children?
- What is the responsibility of schools to teach financial literacy and protect children from overt marketing ploys?
- What role could the government play in protecting children and regulating the three-headed monster?
- What is the role and responsibility of religious organizations in helping young people understand the role money plays in their lives?
- Are colleges/universities doing enough to protect and prepare students for future financial realities?
- What role could relatives play to help shape the balanced financial values of your child?

Chapter SEVEN

Your Own Worst Enemy

We have seen the enemy and they are us.
        —Pogo cartoon by Walt Kelly

Opening Argument in the People's Case against Parents of America:

Parents of America, you have been charged as accomplices in the consumer culture's corrupting of minors. For setting a poor example by overspending, undersaving, and piling on the debt. For being a spending machine and believing that stuff can substitute for quality time with your children. For failing to say no when your children kick into nag mode. For raising financially illiterate children by neglecting to discuss money matters.

I intend to prove beyond a shadow of a doubt that you, Parents of America, have neglected your children's financial values. In doing so, you have allowed the consumer culture—in particular the three-headed monster—to lure your children into a narcissistic lifestyle that encourages unrealistic spending and ignores the needs of others. I am confident that a jury of your grandparents—people who grew up understanding how to balance spending, saving, and sharing—

will find you guilty of failing to teach America's youth to spend wisely, resist temptation, and develop a disciplined use of money.

Exhibit A: Lifestyle Excess

Before you blame all the problems of youth spending on big, bad business and society's failure to protect children, let's take a look at the example set by Parents of America. If youth spending is out of control, could it possibly be in part because parent spending is out of control? Because parents have demonstrated countless times how to buy what you want and not just what you need?

The typical American adult craves all things bigger, better, more convenient or just plain new. Consider the American home. According to the National Association of Home Builders, the average new home built in 1950 was 1100 square feet. Today, new homes average nearly 2200 square feet.[1] Family sizes have shrunk in the past 50 years. Still, Americans have justified doubling the size of their homes. "We are a nation of overspenders, a nation that is into instant-gratification highs," said Olivia Mellan, a Washington, D.C., psychotherapist who specializes in money issues.[2] How else do you explain the growth of suburban subdivisions featuring luxury homes? Dubbed "McMansions" or "starter castles," they feature walk-in closets the size of bedrooms a generation ago.

Americans' lifestyle has escalated so much that PBS produced a special on the subject and named it *Affluenza: The All-Consuming Epidemic*. The writers defined affluenza as "a painful, contagious, socially transmitted condition of overload, debt, anxiety, and waste resulting from the dogged pursuit of more."[3] Parents seem determined to make extravagance the American way of life by choosing the bigger house, trendier clothes, more exotic vacations, and more powerful electronics.

113

Robert H. Frank, professor of Economics at Cornell University, says Americans are caught up in an unrealistic lifestyle of continuous upgrading to improved products, innovations, and more expensive options. In *American Demographics* magazine, he wrote: "While only a tiny fraction of consumers can afford such indulgences (i.e., luxury cars, SUVs, fine jewelry, expensive clothing), this sky's-the-limit up-scaling has raised the stakes for all consumers, sweeping up Americans at every income level into a status spiral that makes the middle-class good life ever more expensive to maintain."[4]

When 71 percent of Americans believe owning an expensive car says, "I've made it," growing numbers of Americans buy cars that make that statement. In the United States, unit sales of luxury vehicles rose 800 percent between 1996 and 2000 compared with a 5 percent rise for ordinary vehicles and light trucks.[5] More people are buying a Mercedes, BMW, Audi, or Lexus, whether they can afford it or not.

In his book, *Luxury Fever: Why Money Fails to Satisfy in an Era of Excess*, Frank says spending on luxury goods is growing four times as fast as overall spending. "As more people buy upscale, the frame of reference that defines what the rest of us consider acceptable will inevitably continue to shift," he writes. "When people at the top spend more, others just below them will inevitably spend more also, and so on all the way down the economic ladder. And as this happens, simpler versions of products that once served perfectly well often fall by the wayside."[6] For example, buying a gas grill for $1000 might seem frugal when the deluxe model sells for $5000, even though it will replace a charcoal grill that cost less than $100.

Frank and others contend that keeping up with the Joneses remains a powerful motivation. However, Americans today tend to compare their lifestyles not with their neighbors but with their higher-paid colleagues or the characters

114

they see on TV. Everybody wants the lifestyle of the rich and famous. As Frank says, "When all of us spend more, the new, higher spending level simply becomes the norm."[7]

For some, "keeping up" is the new American pastime. Greg, a successful management executive, is obsessed with being the first in his circle to own the latest everything. Curiously, the object is almost irrelevant. The high is in the acquisition. New luxury BMW complete with every option possible—check. New, 6000-square-foot home with in-ground pool—check. Fully decked out surround-sound media room—check. Newest model of computer with every accessory imaginable—check. Tens of thousands of dollars thrown around like Monopoly money just to stay ahead of the pack.

Greg doesn't have the money his friends do, but by purchasing big-ticket items before they do, it creates the illusion of equality. What a risky and expensive game of one-upmanship.

Identifying with a more affluent group carries a price tag. According to Juliet Schor, Boston College professor and author of *The Overspent American*, keeping up with the next highest income bracket costs an extra $3000 per year.[8] With their finely tuned compare-o-meters, Americans feel a persistent sense of inadequacy that keeps them spending more than they can afford.

American adults don't even have the sense to know when they have enough. *Affluenza: The All-Consuming Epidemic* attributes the bonanza in self-storage facilities to Americans accumulating more possessions than they can fit in their basements, attics, and garages. Now numbering more than 30,000 operations throughout the country, these rental garage centers have grown fortyfold since the 1960s.[9]

When two-thirds of American households have three TVs or more, excess reigns as normal and has become so ingrained that a downturn in the economy fails to breed caution. Few consumers bothered to hunker down during the recession of 2001 or the stuttering recovery of 2002. Despite the loss of about two million jobs, the steep fall in the stock market, and the September 11 attacks, household spending has defied the traditional pattern and grown every quarter since the recession began.[10] Even with job security and future paychecks on the line, you kept right on spending.

Exhibit B: Consumer Debt

Never before have Americans relied so heavily on money we don't have to buy things we don't need. In the last ten years, the amount of debt on bank credit cards has grown a staggering 163 percent and now totals in excess of $650 billion. More specifically, Americans carried an average credit card balance of $8400 per household in 2002.[11] Using an average interest rate of 15 percent, the typical U.S. family spends more than $1,000 a year to avoid paying cash.

Nothing interrupts America's entrenched spending habits. In the summer of 2001, with the economic slowdown in full swing, 40 percent of Americans admitted to spending more than they earn.[12] The mantra "buy now, pay later" appears so widely accepted that America has grown numb to its potential negative consequences. Going into debt for an education is an investment, but paying a premium of 15 to 20 percent for a night on the town is illogical.

According to the Federal Reserve, household debt is at a record high, relative to disposable income. Some Federal Reserve analysts warn that this unprecedented level of debt might pose a risk to the financial health of American households.

Americans spent so freely during the last recession that record numbers of individuals found themselves in heavy debt and filed for bankruptcy. Personal bankruptcy filings in

2002 rose 15 percent to almost 1.5 million. "Lured by sales, car deals, and low interest rates, consumers spent heartily," said Samuel Gerdano, executive director of the American Bankruptcy Institute.[13]

Ardelle, a rare "live within your means" baby boomer, gave her impression of friends using credit cards by stretching her arms forward, opening her eyes wide and shuffling like a zombie. The set-up was too good, so I asked, as if we were playing charades, "Someone under the spell of hypnotic consumption?" She turned her head, pointed her finger right at me and shouted, "Exactly!"

What impact does the use of credit cards have on young people? A woman in Pennsylvania described how her 7-year-old was shocked to see her buy something with cash. "Mommy, how come you aren't using that plastic card?" she asked. "You buy everything with that card." The mother didn't think her daughter was paying attention to how she used money.

Exhibit C: Savings

As the saying goes, when you shine a light on one area, it casts a shadow on another. In America, debt casts a shadow on savings. Savings as a percentage of after-tax income has plummeted from almost 9 percent in 1992 to barely 3% percent in 2002.[14]

Consider the numbers on saving for college. Today, sending two children to four-year public universities costs $100,222 on average, yet 50 percent of U.S. parents have saved $1,000 or *less* for their children's education. And among those parents who feel *prepared*, fewer than half have saved more than $10,000.[15]

With the dramatic decline, one might expect Americans to be anxious about realities like retirement and financial reserves. *Au contraire*. In a 2002 survey, Americans appeared more confident than in prior years in saving for retirement, even though most have saved only modest amounts and few have adequately planned or prepared for their future needs.

Almost half of all workers admit to having less than $50,000 saved for retirement, while 15 percent say they have saved nothing. Of those ages 40 to 59, only 25 percent have saved $100,000 or more. Ironically, the majority expect to spend at least 20 years in retirement.[16]

Most financial experts agree that retirees will need at least 70 to 80 percent of their pre-retirement income to maintain their current lifestyle. So, if you earn $60,000 a year and plan to retire next year, you need no less than $850,000 invested at 5 percent to meet the 70 percent goal plus another chunk to cover inflation.

In a span of a decade, the nation has forgotten how to save. We seem to have convinced ourselves that we can spend more and worry less about saving. That illusion is a bubble waiting to burst as baby boomers approach retirement age.

For Bob and Sharon, it was easy to justify their spending-no-saving lifestyle. "We both have good jobs, and our house was really appreciating in value," said Bob, a 48-year-old project manager for a construction company. For a while, they saved money in a mutual fund, but when Bob wanted a new boat, bye-bye savings, hello speedboat. When their credit-card debt got out of control, they simply took out a home equity loan and used the money to pay off their bill. While shifting the debt to a lower interest rate made sense, they never changed their runaway consumer habits, so the cycle repeated. "Unfortunately, the home equity angle is so easy to do," said Bob.

Exhibit D: Guilt Money

Parents today spend more time working and commuting and less time being with their children. Despite leisure hours shrinking from 38.2 hours per week in 1993 to 35.3 hours in 1998, Roper Starch Worldwide found that 55 percent of American adults would still choose having more money over having more time. In contrast, 60 percent of kids in America wish they could spend more time with their parents.[17]

Parents reconcile that conflict with guilt money. They choose to climb the ladder of success, then buy more stuff or hand out a bigger allowance as a way to apologize for not being around. According to the BJK&E media report, kids spend about 30 hours of quality time with their parents each year.[18]

"With more parents working and their schedules stretched thin, guilt has settled over American households, and the fallout is a financial bonanza for (young people)," reports the *Christian Science Monitor*. "Cultural rituals, such as increasingly elaborate birthday parties and bar mitzvahs, and high-tab kids' entertainment, such as laser tag and sprawling cineplexes, showcase childhood's escalating cost."[19]

Kids' piggy banks, says Carleton Kendrick, a Boston-based family therapist for LearningNetwork.com, are full of "I'm sorry" money: "I'm sorry I'm not home more. I'm sorry we don't have dinner as a family."[20]

Nick called it a Pokémon emergency. He had made a promise—to be at the band concert or a hockey game or at home by a certain time—and once again had to break it. The next day, he pledged to make it all better by taking his son to the store to pick out yet another pack of Pokémon cards.

Guilt money can play an even more prominent role following a divorce. Mom and dad have one more reason to feel guilty. Sharing custody means less time together, which sometimes spurs parents to spend more freely on their kids. Some also adopt a more generous approach to compete with an ex-spouse.

The easy money for kids has a lot to do with affluenza.

Kendrick says the booming economy of the '90s made it "harder for parents to go out and buy their goodies . . . and then [say no to] kids coming with extended palms and saying, 'What about me?' That's a quantum paradigm shift— kids seeing money virtually as their birthright."[21]

A decade ago, kids ages 8 to 12 earned $6 a week. As of 2000, they averaged $22.68 a week—43 percent from allowance, 25 percent from household chores, 21 percent from parent and grandparent handouts, and 11 percent from work outside the home.[22] Parents spend more money on their kids than ever before, but all the kids really want is more time with Mom and Dad.

Exhibit E: Stress and Money

By spending freely, saving little, and taking on large debt, Americans have increased their risk of money-induced stress. Financial problems cause stress that can endanger relationships, health, and the example parents set for their children.

Few issues cause strain in a relationship like financial disagreements. Study after study lists money as a leading cause of divorce. "I see it over and over—serious relationship tension because couples have different attitudes about how to use money," said Mark, a pastor in Pennsylvania who has talked with hundreds of couples about difficult issues in their marriage. "It starts out with disagreements on small things, like eating out versus eating in, and then escalates into the big-ticket items like cars, trucks, homes, and vacations."

Problems often arise when people don't understand each other's financial habits and values. "As our society has become more materialistic," Mark said, "couples seem to move farther and farther away from a healthy dialogue on the role money plays in their lives."

Research indicates the consumer culture is hazardous to both mental and physical health. Dr. Tim Kasser, an assistant professor of psychology at Knox College, found that people who strongly value wealth and related traits tend to have higher levels of distress, lower levels of well-being, worse relationships, and less connection to their communities.[23]

A study at Ohio State University revealed that people who are stressed about debt, particularly from credit cards, tend to be in worse physical condition. The price of financial anxiety ranges from heart attacks, insomnia, and explosive emotions to difficulty doing such simple tasks as climbing stairs and carrying groceries. "For the individual consumer, this is not a new message," said Paul Lavarakas, director of OSU's Center for Survey Research. "But what's striking is the risk you could be taking down the road with how you manage your debt."[24]

Diane, a self-proclaimed material girl, described how money became a source of stress in her life. "My parents divorced when I was younger," she said. "Because my mom felt guilty, she decided to co-sign for a credit card when I was in high school. Her instructions were to use it wisely." When she and her friends went to the mall, Diane used the card to buy designer clothes that she couldn't afford. "I would brag to my friends that I could buy cool stuff while only making minimum payments," she recalled.

The fun ended and the stress set in as her debt grew bigger and bigger. She lost sleep and worried constantly about her finances. Diane, now 32 and married with one child, works with a therapist on examining her past and current spending behavior. "Although it is one of the hardest things I have done," she said, "I have to get a grip on my actions so I can help my daughter avoid the same pitfalls."

Millions of young people have been in the middle of stress-filled conversations and situations with money playing a starring role. Until parents identify and deal with their stresses related to money, dysfunctional conversations will shape children's perspective on money. And the children will likely struggle with the same issues as their parents.

Exhibit F: Guidance

Not only are parents in arrears on their financial habits, they are transferring their shortcomings to their children. In October of 2002, a national survey of parents discovered that 70 percent said teaching good money habits is essential, yet only 28 percent said they have taught them to their children.[25] Given that enormous gap, should it be a surprise that 40 percent of college students in the United States said money caused tension with family or friends, or that 37 percent said their spending felt out of control?[26]

Sonya, a retail property manager, sheepishly admits getting sucked into the comparison game. "I didn't want my child to have just any old car," she said. "I wanted her to have the best because I knew it would be a direct reflection on our family's success." Sonya surprised her daughter with a brand new SUV for her 17th birthday, and her daughter replied with her own surprise. "She actually said 'Thanks, but why didn't you buy me the sport model in red?' " recalled Sonya.

Not everyone has the means to buy their child an SUV, but the unrealistic consumer expectations you create, no matter the size, reflect a warped form of guidance.

Stephanie, a public relations associate in her mid-20s, feels an undercurrent of competition with her siblings. At family gatherings, they often detail their latest big purchase or exotic travel destination. "In a sick way," said Stephanie, "there is a sense of pride from my parents when one of us describes a significant consumer acquisition. But rarely do they ask if we can afford it." She attributes the odd dynamic to the fact that her family has never talked about realistic ways to approach financial decisions.

The worst kind of guidance is no guidance at all. According to the American Savings Education Council, 31 percent of students say their parents rarely or never discuss setting financial goals with them. Thirty percent report that their parents rarely or never discuss saving and investing with them.[27] Could it be there is nothing to discuss?

Time and again I ask parents how they teach their kids about money. The typical answer begins with nervous laughter followed by silence. In general, they give frequent demonstrations on how to spend, but they rarely discuss saving or sharing.

Too often parents take the easy way out by avoiding the tough stuff: setting ground rules for appropriate financial behavior; living within your means; helping to shape financial values; and establishing a financial philosophy. They don't have these conversations with their kids or for themselves. They fail to share messages of saving for a goal and the joy of sharing. Instead of helping their children learn to manage money for a lifetime of financial health and well-being, they sit there in silence as the consumer culture abducts their children.

Closing Argument

Members of the jury, I have proven beyond a doubt that Parents of America are guilty as charged as accomplices in the consumer culture's corrupting of minors.

In many ways, Parents of America, you are your own worst enemy. You have stood still while marketers suckered you into believing that stuff is a substitute for time. And, try as you might to laugh it off as normal, you have accumulated more consumer debt than at any time in our nation's history. You perpetuate the silence around money that has been passed on for generations. And, as the guilt piles on, so does the stress. In total, these shortcomings suggest you have contributed to the delinquency of a minor.

I have proved the case against Parents of America. And now I recommend a sentence. The harshest penalty would be a lifetime of bailing out your "kid" because he or she has no financial values, no financial skills, and no ability to handle money. Remember, companies hand out credit cards like candy at Halloween—even to unemployed college students—because you "come to the rescue" whenever collection agencies start calling. Like it or not, for the rest of your days, you may hear perpetual requests for money because you are your child's ATM.

There is an alternative. With your child's financial future at a critical juncture, you can choose to change. I believe that you care about your child and have made mistakes without knowing the consequences. The first step is to admit that you have a problem and recognize that you may have to alter some deeply ingrained habits. By acknowledging your shortcomings, you can change your child's future one day at a time, one conversation at a time, and one reevaluated consumer decision at a time.

Whichever direction you choose, you need to know that your decision probably will impact your family for generations to come.

The choice is yours.

Parents of America, what say you?

Money Talks

- Have you ever found yourself in dogged pursuit of more?
- Have you ever lived beyond your means in hopes of being viewed by your peers as more accomplished on the status ladder than you really are?

- Grade your effort in shaping your child's financial values and in teaching them critical financial skills. (Use the letter scale A through F.)
- Are you concerned about your financial future?
- Do you think your current financial habits will have an impact on your children?
- If you reviewed your savings history over the last several years with your grandparents, what would they say?
- Do you justify spending more time at work because it affords you the opportunity to buy more stuff?
- Do you use money and/or stuff to numb the effects of lost time?
- Do you worry the pattern has created unrealistic expectations on the part of your child?
- Can you identify with Diane in any way?
- Have issues of money been a source of stress and tension in your relationships?
- Do you have a solid financial foundation (i.e., healthy financial values and boundaries) that you can count on in times of stress?
- Will you be a better role model as you teach your child to balance spending, saving, and sharing?
- Will you make the necessary changes in your own consumer habits?
- Will you demand more (or less) of other influencers in the village so you don't have to go it alone?

Part TWO

A Better Way

Chapter EIGHT

Money See, Money Do

As a parent, you're on your own. You may feel over-whelmed and outmaneuvered. After all, it's you against billions of dollars in ads and promotions, sophisticated brainpower aimed at mind control, almighty peer pressure, and societal momentum toward excess. And you'll probably get little help from the rest of the village. Not exactly the ideal environment for teaching good financial habits.

But you are your child's primary hope for overcoming a possession-crazed society. No one else cares the way you do, has so much invested—emotionally and financially—in your child, and can see how your child is affected.

You talk to your kids about so many things. Now start having frequent, intentional conversations about money. It's up you to initiate the conversation and to set financial boundaries and priorities and to teach healthy financial habits. Who else will tell them to save up for that big purchase, to wait a few weeks because it might go on sale, to consider getting more value with an off-brand, to "just say no" to another pair of shoes? Who else will help them establish the discipline to save for a long-term goal or experience the joy of sharing money and time with a cause they are passionate about?

Here's the shocker: Your kids will listen! Seventy-five percent of American children say they have learned the most about how to manage money from their parents.[1] They'll listen intently when you tell them they're being manipulated. Nothing infuriates independence-hungry young people like the idea that somebody's trying to play them. The key question: What can you do with this opportunity?

If you think about your own habits and actions relative to money, the simple concept of money see, money do has powerful implications. As with other learned behaviors, many of your child's financial habits will mirror your daily

Parent Power

Parents play the pivotal role in shaping a child's financial habits and values. In 2000, a survey by Yankelovich Partners for Lutheran Brotherhood asked American adults what most influenced them to spend, save, or share when they were learning about money as a child. Table 8.1 illustrates their response.

Table 8.1 Influences on Financial Habits

	Spending (%)	Saving (%)	Sharing (%)
Parents and family	43	81	61
Friends and peers	18	3	3
Media (TV, radio, newspapers or magazines)	13	1	4
Family's income	9	4	2
Place of worship	1	1	14

Source: A national survey by Yankelovich Partners for Lutheran Brotherhood (now known as Thrivent Financial for Lutherans).

130

and weekly routine. Looking back, I certainly found that to be true in my case.

My parents frequently talked about how they saved money and also what causes they supported. Even when they contemplated certain spending decisions, like a car or new furniture, I remember it being part of the family dialogue. I know some of my habits were influenced by what I heard and observed. Remember, in the right context, imitation is the greatest form of flattery.

Getting Started

Lots of good books tell you how to teach your kids to manage money, but few books help you get ready for some of the most vitally important conversations about money you and your child will ever have. By taking the time now, you may save yourself countless hours of frustration, wondering what happened to your kids and where you went wrong.

This chapter will help you understand the "why" behind your actions and decisions with money. I hope it will help you strengthen your money teaching skills, become a better role model and refine your current approach. In some instances, you might need to consider making a change in your thinking and behavior. Ultimately, that's for you to decide.

Many of the parents I've talked with eventually realized they didn't have an approach or a philosophy for teaching their kids about money. I recommend a six-step process that prepares you for a wide variety of financial conversations. Just as an aspiring musician, athlete, or chef improves by building on a foundation of skills, so too will this process help you develop a foundation and routine as you teach your child about money.

Think of yourself as a player-coach. Although most often used in the sporting world, the term could apply to an orchestra conducted by one of its own or a chef-owned restaurant. Regardless of the field, the role can be tricky. Not only do you have to keep your skills sharp, you must provide quality leadership.

So, what will it take? The essentials include a commitment to obtaining a healthy, balanced routine; mastery of some basic financial concepts, and a positive frame of mind in conversations with your child. We all know that talking and teaching about money can be difficult. But, using this process, the experience can be rewarding, possibly even life-altering.

I recommend spending time on these steps. This is important preparation for the lessons and suggestions that follow. As you set aside some time to go through the process you might experience a newfound energy for present and future financial conversations.

Step 1: Look Back

To understand the significance of your role, step back and think about when you first learned about money. This step is so critical because we often replicate what and how we learn. The "money memories" that play over and over in your head can be a powerful force in shaping your approach with your own child. Let me offer a few questions for you to consider. Think back to when you were growing-up:

- Did your parents talk with you about money?
- What specific situations do you remember that showed how your parents used their money?
- Which of your parents' actions with money did you copy?
- Which do you still copy?
- If your parents had a financial philosophy that guided their overall approach to money, how would you define it?
- In what ways were your parents' attempts to teach you about money helpful?

- Where did they fall on the "Goldilocks" spectrum: too controlling, too lenient, or just right?
- In what ways were your parents good role models for using money?

If two parents live in the house, I recommend you discuss these questions together. If someone answers yes while the other answers no, talk it through so it doesn't become a barrier in role modeling. Insight into each other's background will prove invaluable as you either prepare or press on in teaching your kids about money. Discussing these things early in your relationship contributes to long-term success in teaching your child. Remember, what you do with money is an extension of who you are and what you believe and, for your kids, who they will ultimately become.

What may seem like a trivial memory can be critical insight to how you teach. Susan, a 45-year-old family therapist with two kids, told me about her earliest memories of how her parents used money. "We never talked about money. It was one of those unspoken subjects," she said. "In fact, when we would go out to eat, my dad would pay the bill by opening his wallet under the table without letting any of us, my mom included, see how much the bill was or how much money he had."

I have heard hundreds of stories like Susan's. Adults of all ages have shared with me how awkward their family conversations and situations were around money. Although Susan is in her mid-40s, she remembers the moment like it was yesterday. This is a powerful reminder of how your actions will influence your child.

Susan said she works hard to use the awareness of those situations to guide her actions with money around her kids. Now, when she and her kids are eating out or shopping, she makes a point to include them in the discussion of how much things cost. Susan admits she may go overboard in talking to them about financial matters. But she is determined not to repeat her father's method, so she opts for showing the many different things she does with money. I commended her on breaking the cycle.

By understanding how you learned to use money, your odds for success in teaching healthy financial habits and values improve dramatically.

Step 2: Begin Identifying Your Financial Values

The next step in the process is to understand what values drive your money decisions. Your financial values are the beliefs and priorities that guide your financial decisions. In turn, they play a significant role in shaping your children's outlook.

Your best opportunity for helping your child escape the spell of hypnotic consumption is to define, understand, and then formulate a plan with balanced financial values. To do that, you need to do the following:

- Know your strengths and your weaknesses.
- Understand the difference between a need and a want within your given value system.
- Review your current routine of talking about money and evaluate its effectiveness.

Basic needs in life are quite simple: clothing, food, shelter, and transportation. Most everything else is a want. However, these can vary greatly, depending on your value system. Because this is such a major step, I devote all of Chapter 9 to financial values.

Step 3: Have Effective Financial Discussions

"Americans believe in life, liberty, and the purchase of happiness." Although meant in jest, this quip carries a hint of truth, especially when you consider our financially overextended ways. If you see yourself in that statement, it is important that before engaging your child on the topic you review your own habits first. Chapter 11 is devoted entirely to helping you accomplish that goal.

To set the table for productive and meaningful conversations, consider a few keys.

1. *Start Now.* The three-headed monster will not ask your permission and will start trying to shape your child's financial values as early as 18 months of age.[2] I have been asked at least a thousand times, "When do I start talking to my child about money?" Do not wait until your child reaches puberty to stumble into the subject. To offset the effect of marketing, you need to start early and establish a routine. A simple rule of thumb: By the time your child can say "I want," you should be keenly aware of the messages your child gets from you and the surrounding environment.

2. *Start Talking.* Talking about money may be more difficult than discussing sex or drugs. Many parents have said there is an abundance of literature to help break the ice on sex and drugs, but precious little on talking to your kids about money. There are many factors that come into play when teaching about money. But it still means you need to take the first step. Teach from a proactive instead of a reactive position.

3. *Walk the Walk.* Avoid the "do as I say, not as I do" approach. It rarely works and merely undermines your credibility. If your children see you buying all the latest gadgets, trendy brand name clothes, and eating at expensive restaurants, while barely paying the minimum on your credit card balances, you will have difficulty with the "live within your means" speech. Chapter 13 goes into more detail on this topic. As with any good mentoring relationship, acknowledging your own occasional misstep can be a healthy part of your kid's learning process.

4. *Be Intentional*. Establish a rhythm and a frequency for your conversations. The people who have the most success with these money talks keep it simple. "We try to look for teachable moments with our kids," said Gwen, a mother of kids age seven and five. "Something easy, like talking about the extra amount you pay for brand names over generic and then discussing if it's really worth it." For example, Gwen picked out two similar food items in the grocery store and set up a blind taste test on brand name versus generic for her kids. "It was a fun and easy way to teach a lesson on value," she said. She recommends doing this with an item not regularly on the shopping list so the kids aren't predisposed to a certain flavor.

Other parents have had similar success with clothing. Kathleen, a single mom of three, has worked hard to help her kids steer clear of wearing logo-plastered clothing. "I told them that, by wearing clothing with overt logos, such as Tommy Girl, the company essentially uses them as a billboard for free advertising. So, unless the company pays them to endorse their stuff, bye-bye logos."

Have her kids, ages 14, 11, and 10, resisted the rule? "Not once," she said. To her credit, she has also spent considerable time reinforcing the message that the clothes don't make the person. Bottom line, she has helped them understand the difference between ad hype and feeling good about who they are without succumbing to brand pressure.

I like both approaches because each illustrates the concept of using teachable moments. When I talk about having frequent, intentional conversations, it means taking advantage of opportunities that are in front of you every day to help shape your kid's financial values. Maybe you explain that, in buying a cheaper car with excellent gas mileage, you save money on gasoline, insurance, and car payments, thereby allowing you to save more in your child's college fund. Not to mention that it is friendlier to the environment. Or occasionally mention that going out to eat costs "x" times more than staying home and cooking it yourself. The point isn't to make it complicated, but to be intentional.

More food for thought: Whenever possible, compliment your kids when you observe them exercising good financial judgment. Kathleen told me how excited her 14-year-old daughter was that she waited to buy something until it went on sale. "The item only cost $10, but the point was she used good judgment and I congratulated her for making a good decision," said a proud Kathleen.

Again, I am not suggesting you turn everything into a financial lesson. If you do, your kids are sure to revolt. But don't be surprised if it feels like your primary role is that of counter-rhythm to the hypnotic beat of consumer messages. Remember, few members of the village participate in or support your quest for financial balance.

Step 4: Set Limits

The Power Behind Saying No

Setting healthy limits and establishing appropriate financial boundaries for your kids can be challenging. As discussed earlier, you have many forces working against you—from the siren song of excess to the guilty feelings that lead to substituting time with stuff. For some, setting limits may parallel the experience of learning a foreign language.

Perhaps some of you remember the experience of sitting in the language lab, trying to form your mouth to utter even the simplest of words. The same could be true as you practice saying the word "no." It may feel awkward at first, but understanding the importance of the word cannot be understated. When you say yes, it requires no explanation. When you say no, it could mean several uncomfortable minutes defending your position and holding your ground.

The key to establishing healthy financial boundaries is

to have certain guidelines and expectations that are supported with consistent behavior. The following questions will help analyze your current approach:

- Can your child buy anything with his or her money, or are certain things off limits?
- Is there a maximum amount of money your child can spend at one time?
- Does your child observe you being fiscally responsible?
- Do you ever say no now and yes later to the same request?

Setting boundaries early, then sticking to them sets an important tone for present and future lessons on money. A word of caution: Don't say you can't afford something if you really can because your kids will look back later and realize it wasn't true. Try saying, "It costs too much and is not within our value system." The opposite is true as well. Don't pretend you can afford something if you really can't. The long-term message sent to your child will be, "It's okay to live beyond your means."

By establishing a reasonable list of expectations and guidelines, you create necessary structure in your approach. One reason the marketing machine succeeds in separating people from their money is that millions of Americans have a very loose structure in how they use their money.

When you take the time to set limits, you become more conscious of your surroundings and can do a better job of guiding your child. And, when there are the inevitable disagreements, you'll have a solid foundation to support your stand.

Barbara, an affluent parent of three, described a recent boundary challenge with her 15-year-old daughter. "Tracy went to the mall with a friend and before she left we agreed that she was not to buy anything. When she returned home, she tried to hide a bag from me by quickly heading to her room," said Barbara. Even though it wasn't the most convenient time, the situation demanded immediate attention.

Barbara then described her quandary, "Do I blow it off or do I address it to reinforce a lesson of restraint and the agreement we had." She decided to ask Tracy what was in the bag. No surprise, it was a shirt from Tracy's favorite clothing store.

Barbara expressed her displeasure and offered a choice: "You can either return the shirt to the store or donate it to a charity." Tracy chose the former. Another factor in Barbara's decision was that Tracy's sisters were watching the situation unfold. "I knew that how I handled the issue would affect not only Tracy, but her sisters as well." When it comes to money, the best decision isn't always the easy decision.

Step 5: Silence the Nag Factor

It was supposed to be a simple trip to the grocery store. Jeff needed some items to get ready for the week and his 7-year-old son, Ryan, was in tow. What should have been an 30-minute errand turned into a world-class temper tantrum. "I should have seen it coming," said Jeff. "From the moment we climbed in the car, Ryan was bugging me to buy a sugared cereal that he knew I wouldn't get. Even though I said no, he kept on asking, thinking I would cave. When we turned down the cereal aisle, and I said no for probably the tenth time, he lost it. Crying, whining, accusing me of not loving him—he tried every angle."

What parent hasn't been in that unfortunate situation when your child's want becomes the center of the universe.

In the book, *The Kids Market: Myths and Realities*, Dr. James McNeal, summarizes the changes that have occurred in parental response to children's requests from the early 1980s to the mid 1990s:

1980—No: "Don't nag me. I know what's best for you."

1990—Maybe: "All right, I hear you. I'll consider it."

1995—Yes: "I understand you prefer that. I'll get it when I go shopping if I can find it on sale."[3]

McNeal says that today's family lifestyle assumes parents expect purchase requests from kids and that most will be accepted and fulfilled. He details the number of requests made by children ages 4 to 12:

- About 15 requests per shopping trip with parents.
- About 5 requests a day at home.
- About 10 requests a day on vacation.[4]

McNeal says children total about 3000 product and service requests a year, and parents honor these requests 50 percent of the time.[5] When you pull out the calculator and add it all up, that can be big money! Perhaps now it is clear why auto manufacturers advertise in kid magazines.

When Parents Say Yes

To what extent do parents honor requests made by children ages 8 to 12?

Product	Percentage of Requests Honored
School Supplies	80
Vacation Venue	75
Shoes	70
Software	70
Clothes	60
Soft Drinks	60
Toiletries	60

Product	Percentage of Requests Honored
Cookies	50
Candy	45
Toys	40

Source: Dr. James U. McNeal. ©1999 Paramount Market Publishing, Inc., Ithaca, New York.

Take a look at the list on how often parents grant requests for specific products. According to McNeal, the percentage of requests granted is in inverse proportion to the number of times a child asked for an item in that category. In other words, items requested the most times, such as toys, were least likely to be granted.[6] The list should prove helpful on two fronts: first, to help you understand the magnitude and diversity of children's requests and, second, to overwhelmingly reinforce the need for a strategy to counter the nag.

Silencing the nag factor has been a priority for Eric and Tracy. As parents of three energetic boys, ages 3, 6, and 7, they work hard to set limits and say no when it would be easier to give in. As the boys' uncle, I witnessed this first hand when I traveled with them to Walt Disney World. Even though virtually every ride ends by dumping you in a gift shop, the boys never shifted into nag mode. Not exactly the outcome Disney hopes for.

One key to their success: establishing good habits from the beginning. "We felt that by deciding early on not to give in to their requests, we could avoid the trap others may fall into," said Eric. The trap he is referring to is what happens when you establish a pattern of saying yes. The child can become so conditioned to getting his way that reversing course proves challenging.

Eric and Tracy have also transferred financial choices to the two older boys. "On the rare occasion they do start bugging us for something, I remind them they have money and then ask if that's what they want to spend it on," Eric explained. Sounds simple, but the success lies in the follow-through.

If the trend is to give kids more decision-making influence, parents need to be on guard against the thousands of requests they face each year. Experts say that intermittent positive reinforcement only serves to strengthen the child's undesirable behavior. The earlier you establish boundaries and ground rules for making consumer decisions, the more successful you will be in teaching your kids lessons on sharing, saving, and spending.

Step 6: Allow Financial Mistakes

One of the most important things you can do as kids learn to use money is to know when to intervene and when to hang back. What parent hasn't cringed as she watches her child exercise questionable financial judgment or irresponsibly lose track of a possession?

Karen, a grade school counselor for over 20 years and a mother of two, has facilitated many parenting classes for families in her school. One question comes up repeatedly: What do you do when a child has been irresponsible and lost something nonessential, like a toy or sports equipment? "If the child has left it out in the rain or it got stolen because it wasn't put away, resist the temptation to run to the store and replace it at the drop of a hat," Karen says. "Instead, consider having a conversation with your child about the consequences of their behavior." Good advice.

Understanding consequences for one's actions related to money is important to learn at a young age. A lack of that understanding can lead to a lifetime of stress and difficulty with financial struggles.

Teri, a newspaper columnist in her late 20s, described to me how unfortunate it was that she never learned the value of money or the negative implications of making questionable financial decisions. Teri grew up in a relatively wealthy family and was never counseled about her financial choices. "I have no memory of my parents telling me if my decisions were good, bad, or otherwise. They gave me money, and I spent it," she said. "When I got to college, I kept spending like I was living at home, only now I was using a credit card. I had no clue how to make good financial decisions. The only reason I changed is three years into my job, I faced the decision of filing bankruptcy or working with a credit counselor to pay off my debt." Although Teri has been working hard to right her financial ship without parental involvement, one wonders if she could have avoided those problems with good coaching.

Observing your child's emerging financial habits provides ongoing opportunities for teaching financial values. Young people tend to get sucked into the trap of impulse buying. What kid hasn't given in to the immediate desire to buy the latest trend toy?

For me, it was the handheld Mattel electronic football game popular back in the '70s. I saw it, I wanted it, and I bought it with my money and with my parents' knowledge. Compared to the super-realistic video games of today, this game was closer to Xs and Os on a chalkboard. Essentially, it was a bunch of blinking lines on a tiny little screen powered by a D battery. It held my attention for about two weeks. The next turn of events was one small way my parents helped me learn about the consequences of buying something on impulse.

I remember approaching my dad and asking if I could return the game to the store because it wasn't fun anymore. First he said, "No, that wouldn't be right." Then he explained to me that, even though we often want to buy something right then, sometimes it's best to wait a day or so and think about it.

What a simple but important life lesson on the difference between immediate and deferred gratification. In the scheme of things, my mistake wasn't a big deal, but that few moments of guidance, along with other similar lessons on financial values, has served me well.

Building Confidence

When it comes to issues of money management, whether it's the good, the bad, or the ugly, it's all in the family. So much of what your child learns about appropriate financial behavior comes from the people they look up to most—Mom and Dad. If you seriously want to teach your child about healthy financial boundaries, you'll find it helpful to examine your own skills as you go. If you learn something along the way, you'll be even better able to guide your child. After all, confidence is contagious.

Your mini-lessons and encouragement will help your child establish the confidence to be money wise. And your gift of persistence, even when it seems like you aren't getting through, will be rewarded in the end. Remember, the strongest defense against the consumer culture is kids who learn to accept themselves for who they are.

Money Talks

- Which of your financial habits and values do you want to pass on to your child?
- Which of your financial habits and values would you not want your child to imitate?

- How effective is your approach in handling the nag factor?
- Are you consistent in your approach to teaching about money?
- Are you too controlling, too permissive, or just right in setting financial boundaries?

Chapter NINE

Your Money, Your Values

I am so convinced that having healthy financial boundaries is paramount to your child's financial future that this entire chapter addresses this topic. It's about bringing consistency to your heart and your wallet. By creating a financial philosophy that is right for you, you increase the probability of your child having a prosperous life.

The best tool for teaching your child about money is financial values. By this, I mean the beliefs and priorities that guide your financial decisions. Defining our values, especially as it relates to money, is a forgotten art. In a recent survey of kids by the Tiger Woods Foundation, only 19 percent of kids said they spend much time thinking about values.

What about your own values? Do you spend time reflecting on your own financial habits and assess whether they accurately reflect your beliefs and priorities? Given the increased consumer onslaught, it requires more diligence than ever to maintain healthy financial boundaries.

Charles, a successful entrepreneur, is the epitome of "work hard to play hard." He grew up working in the successful family business. There he was taught the importance of saving for the future and participated with his family in giving back to charity—both time and money. He and his wife, Cathy, are committed, caring parents, but they have not passed on similar financial values to their kids.

Charles and Cathy both admit having erred in believing that stuff is a substitute for time. Consider the kids' playroom. It is loaded with every video game and electronic gadget imaginable. Gone are the days of saving for the future and sharing resources with worthy causes. Present are the days devoted to material goods and exotic travel.

I share their situation to highlight how easy it is for a family to short-circuit its financial values. This dramatic shift took just one generation. With no one and no process to help Charles and Cathy revisit their core values, their early financial boundaries were obliterated. I think this phenomenon is more common than we realize.

Little compromises here and there seem inconsequential, but they all add up to significant impact. You can point the finger of blame in many directions. When you combine a climate of hyper-consumer activity along with whirlwind schedules for parents, the by-product is a tornado of confusion and misdirection. If we aren't there already, the erosion of financial values could soon be epidemic.

Let's revisit a study by the Center for a New American Dream, which found that 87 percent of parents feel that advertising and marketing aimed at children makes kids too materialistic. Parents also said advertising and marketing hurt kids' self-esteem, damage their values and world view, and cause many parents to work longer hours to pay for things their children feel they need.[1]

My counter: Parents with strong financial values can neutralize the hypnotic force of excess. Values are the cornerstone for shaping balanced financial boundaries. Taken seriously, well-defined values will be your rock of Gibraltar in the quicksand of consumerism. Values can even silence the endless drone of the nag factor by helping you set a consistent standard.

This chapter is designed to be highly interactive—from a quiz that will help you assess your current financial habits to questions that will help you ponder the whys behind your actions. It is my hope that you will gain clarity about the ever-present responsibility of teaching by example as well as discover critical insight for maintaining healthy financial boundaries.

Financial Reality Check

Checkups are a normal part of our routine. Maybe it's an annual physical, a regular visit to the dentist, or taking your car in for an oil change. Regardless, paying attention to the little things often works as good insurance for the future. In all of these cases, an ounce of prevention is worth a pound of cure.

No surprise, it's also true with our financial habits. Just as the doctor tells us to watch our eating and exercise habits, so too we need a friendly reminder to pay attention to our financial habits. Unfortunately, slip-ups are both easy and justifiable.

Consider what you are up against. "There are some things in life money can't buy, for everything else there's MasterCard"—brilliantly designed ads make overspending seem so fun and innocent. Like it or not, seductive messages of excess try to erode your financial boundaries on a 24-7 schedule. Given the repetitive chant of the consumer culture, periodically reviewing your financial habits is essential for maintaining balance.

I believe establishing and maintaining healthy financial boundaries depends on two key components: good habits and a values-infused decision-making process.

The first exercise is designed to help you assess your current financial habits. Take a few minutes to answer the questions because the more familiar you are with how you use money, the better you will be at carving out your financial philosophy.

Financial Habits Checkup

1. Do you currently carry a balance on a credit card?   Yes_____   No_____

2. In the past year, have you ever paid only the minimum due on a credit card?   Yes_____   No_____

3. Do you currently have more than three active credit cards?   Yes_____   No_____

4. Do you use a cash card more than once a week?   Yes_____   No_____

5. Is your mortgage payment (principal and interest) more than 30 percent of your annual household income?   Yes_____   No_____

6. Do you think at least weekly about your next large discretionary purchase?   Yes_____   No_____

7. Do you have a garage, basement, or attic filled with stuff you don't use?   Yes_____   No_____

8. Do you rent a storage space for things you rarely use?   Yes_____   No_____

9. In the past six months, have you gone shopping to lift your spirits?   Yes_____   No_____

10. Are you currently behind in paying any of your bills?   Yes_____   No_____

11. In the last year, have you lost sleep worrying about money?   Yes_____   No_____

12. Have you paid a late fee on a credit card in the last year?   Yes_____   No_____

13. Do you own or lease vehicles whose total sticker price exceeds 50 percent of your annual income?   Yes_____   No_____

14. In the last year, has money caused tension in your relationship with your spouse or kids?   Yes_____   No_____

15. Do you currently gamble or buy lottery tickets in hopes of improving your financial situation?   Yes_____   No_____

(Continued)

Financial Habits Checkup *(Continued)*

16. Have you adequately protected yourself with disability and life insurance? (A rule of thumb for basic coverage: 60 percent of your annual income for disability coverage and 10 times your annual income for life insurance) Yes_____ No_____

17. Do you at least weekly give in to your child's request for a purchase? Yes_____ No_____

18. Do you consider how your financial actions and decisions (i.e., how you spend, save, and share your money) impact your child? Yes_____ No_____

19. Do you follow a budget (doesn't have to be fancy)? Yes_____ No_____

20. Do you have nonretirement savings equal to three to six months of income? Yes_____ No_____

21. Do you contribute at least 6 percent of your income to a retirement account? Yes_____ No_____

22. Do you save ahead for large expenses, like a vacation and holiday spending, to avoid accumulating debt on a credit card? Yes_____ No_____

23. Do you designate a specific percentage or dollar amount each year for charity? Yes_____ No_____

24. Do you have specific financial goals (i.e., I want to save "x" for a down payment on a home, I want to save "y" for my child's college education, I want a portion of my beneficiary designation to go to charity)? Yes_____ No_____

25. Do you talk about money with your spouse/ partner/kids at least once a week? Yes_____ No_____

How to Score:

Questions 1–17, every yes answer is worth two points.
Questions 18–25, every no answer is worth two points.
If it's too close to call, give yourself one point.

0–10   Good work, your habits appear healthy, your financial outlook balanced.

11–20   Caution, you may need to rethink some habits.

21–35   Warning, your habits are heading into a potential danger area. Strongly encourage reevaluation and close monitoring.

36–50   Alert, serious need to reevaluate how you use money. Seek a competent professional for assistance. (See National Foundation for Credit Counseling—www.nfcc.org.)

The Financial Habits Checkup is designed to help you identify your current financial habits and priorities. You will probably see both strengths and weaknesses in your answers. Everyone has patterns with how they use money. But do we spend enough time thinking about their current and future impact?

The challenge and the opportunity are to periodically review your financial goals and objectives. If you review the entries in your checkbook for the last six months, it will reveal a lot about your financial priorities. When you combine the pace of our society with the overwhelming pull to spend, the result can be disastrous. The ease and speed at which a person can fall out of balance is remarkable. If your score is higher than you expected, don't be discouraged. Rather, be encouraged by your desire to improve your situation.

Financial Values Reflection

The next exercise will help you contemplate life's bigger questions on why you use money the way you do. For some, this will be familiar territory. For others, it may feel awkward. Just like the checkup, this exercise is an important step in shaping your financial philosophy. While some questions can be answered quickly, others may take a few hours or even a few days to fully explore.

This exercise incorporates some of history's most revered thinkers, a reminder that people have been thinking and talking about money, possessions, and values for thousands of years. The fact that money and possessions are leading topics in the Bible, Torah, Koran, and other religious teachings shows that people have been struggling with financial priorities and need guidance. It also demonstrates that the need for financial values is universal.

If you are married, consider doing the exercise together. It will help pinpoint areas where you and your spouse differ. Take the time to talk about those differences so you understand each other's thinking, which should help alleviate tension in your financial discussions. You may also want to record your thoughts to use as a springboard for future conversations. Consider the effect your answers have on your children. After all, you are their teacher, role model, and mentor.

What Is Most Important to You?

Manifest plainness,
Embrace simplicity,
Reduce selfishness,
Have few desires.
There is no calamity greater than lavish desires.
There is no greater guilt than discontentment.
And there is no greater disaster than greed.
　　　—Lao Tzu, Father of Taoism (c. 604–c. 531 B.C.)[2]

This question is fundamental to what you value. In the fall of 2000, we asked several thousand middle-school kids and their parents this same question. The workshop, called "Your Money, Your Message," discussed the role money plays in their lives.

I wanted the kids to think about what was truly important to them, not what someone else—advertisers, peers, TV stars—said it should be. Judging from the looks of parents in the room, many were pleasantly surprised to hear their kids' answers. By spending time on this question, you may surprise yourself, too. Make a list. Anything goes.

What Is Your Personal Financial Plan?

It is thrifty to prepare today for the wants of tomorrow.
　　　—The Ant and the Grasshopper, Aesop (fl. c. 550 B.C.)[3]

Some people spend more time planning their annual vacation than planning their financial future. I have encountered many individuals who intend to create a financial plan but always seem to save it for tomorrow. It may not be as fun as a day at the lake with your kids, but when it comes to important financial tasks, it should be at the top of the list. If you find it difficult to tackle, you are not alone.

More people don't plan than do. To plan means facing the truth about how you use your money. Creating a roadmap for your present and your future is critical to establishing balanced financial values. You may think, "What if I've never done that before?" Chapters 10 through 14 will help you formulate or reinforce your financial philosophy. From there, you can budget and set priorities with values in mind. It doesn't have to be complicated, but it should be written down.

A common mistake: focusing all your energy on investment goals. Give attention first to the basics—life and disability insurance, an emergency fund equal to three to six months of income, and a values-based budget.

Consider Your Priorities on Sharing, Saving, and Spending

Living a balanced life means leaving the womb of easy existence and entering into a partnership with God dedicated to sustaining the world, to making it productive, to reaping its benefits, to making it all it can be.
—Jeffrey K. Salkin , Senior Rabbi, The Community Synagogue, Port Washington, New York[4]

I believe these three words capture all that you can do with money:

Share: Give money away to someone or some organization that is important to you.

Save: Put money in reserve for short- and long-term goals. I consider investing a subset of saving.

Spend: Exchange money for products and services, both those you need and those you want.

Now, let's make this more interesting. Out of the blue, someone hands you a check for $100,000. First, consider how you would allocate the money to each category (i.e., 15 percent to sharing, 25 percent to saving, 60 percent to spending). Then, determine the "why" behind your decision.

After you have pondered this opportunity, invite your child to consider the same question using a smaller denomination ($100 or, perhaps, $1,000). Then, after you have explained the rational for your percentages, ask your child to do the same. This simple exercise is sure to inspire lively conversation and debate about your respective financial priorities. In later chapters, I'll offer additional suggestions to build on the theme of sharing, saving, and spending.

How Can You Make Financial Decisions That Support the People, Places, and Things That Matter to You Most?

> *Do all the good you can,*
> *By all the means you can,*
> *In all the ways you can,*
> *In all the places you can,*
> *At all the times you can,*
> *To all the people you can,*
> *As long as you ever can.*
> —John Wesley, founder of the
>   Methodist Church (1703–1791)[5]

Refer to your answer to the first question, What is most important to you? Focus on the big picture, not the precise details. For example, if you know you want to build a college fund, consider how much you spend on buying or leasing a new car. If you want quality time with your family, weigh the implications of taking a higher paying job with more time demands. Unless carefully monitored, some financial decisions can conflict with what's important to you.

Remember the financial values meltdown of Charles

and Cathy earlier in this chapter? They are good people who love their kids, but they eventually substituted quality time with stuff. Their actions conflicted with their basic values.

If this approach is new to you, revisit this question monthly to determine if your strategy is still on course. It's been said that it takes 21 days to form a habit. Ideally, your big decisions will filter down and begin to influence your day-to-day financial activities.

How Will Saving an Adequate Amount for Future Needs Improve Your Financial Outlook Today?

Industry, Perseverance, and Frugality, make Fortune Yield.
—Poor Richard's Almanack[6]

When people plan for long-term financial goals, they minimize their financial stress. Why? Because they are addressing their future needs. If you have never addressed the issue of long-term saving (i.e., house, retirement), seek out a financial adviser or search the Internet, where you will find a myriad of helpful tools. As you mull over this question, weigh the differences between immediate gratification and deferred gratification, and consider how little encouragement you get to do the latter.

You can learn a lot by talking with retired people who have drastically changed their lifestyle because they lack adequate retirement funds. Determining the appropriate amount you should be saving depends on your goals and objectives. Be on guard against undersaving because of your wants today. As you plan, keep in mind that, according to the National Center for Health Statistics, the average life expectancy for men in the U.S. is 73.8 years and for women is 79.5 years.

Do You Think It Is Important to Save for Major Expenditures Like Cars, Furniture, and Vacations?

That man is the richest whose pleasures are the cheapest.
—Henry David Thoreau[7]

155

Resist the temptation to move past this question too quickly. I challenge you to stop and think about the implication of your answer. Easy credit gives us access to things we may never have dreamed of acquiring, such as exotic vacations, big screen TVs and expensive SUVs. It's one thing to have the money for your vacation and choose to use the 60 days until the bill is due to pay it in full. It's quite another to pay an extra 20-plus percent to the credit card company for the loveseat you just had to have today. Leasing a vehicle is similar in that a larger monthly payment may be easier to justify if you don't have to part with thousands of dollars upfront.

How you answer this question speaks fundamentally to your financial habits. When you set a goal and save money for something you really want, you are living within your means. If you routinely spend money on things you can't afford, it's time to reevaluate your decisions—especially if you compromise on short- and long-term financial basics, like insurance and an emergency fund. How would your grandparents have answered this question?

Should You Have a Percentage of Your Income in a Short-Term Savings Account for Emergency Use?

A fool and his money are soon parted.
—Anonymous English Proverb[8]

Again, it may seem like an easy one to answer, but the key is in the follow-through. For some, the temptation of having cash sitting in an easily accessible account is unbearable. For the three-headed monster, it's low-hanging fruit. How would you handle having that money around? Most financial experts agree that it should be three to six months' worth of income.

Life is full of unexpected events—a short-term disability, an unexpected job loss, or a sick relative. Few people go through life without some kind of incident. By having an adequate amount of money stored away, you can minimize your financial hardship.

Do You Share Some of Your Income with Charitable Organizations?

No act of kindness, no matter how small, is ever wasted.
—*The Lion and the Mouse*, Aesop (fl. c. 550 B.C.)[9]

As you contemplate this question, consider the following. For the first time in almost a decade, the number of people living in poverty in the United States has increased. The needs of others around the world, especially in developing countries, are as great as they have ever been. Our country has a rich history of reaching out to others in need whether locally or globally. One way you can ensure that tradition will continue is to role model giving in your own family. By sharing the reasons behind your philanthropic decisions, your children will begin to experience the joy of giving.

If you wiped the slate clean, how much stuff would you really need to be happy? Have there been causes that you wanted to support, but just didn't think you could afford to? In our consumer-frenzy society, the overwhelming message we hear is that having more stuff equates to some odd measure of success. Perhaps after 9/11 our view is beginning to change.

What Is the Value of Having a Budget?

Beware of little expenses; a small leak will sink a great ship.
—Poor Richards Almanack[10]

Notice, I don't insist that you have a budget. Rather I ask you to consider the *value* of having a budget. Too often people cringe when someone mentions the "B" word. Like it's going to mean you can't have fun anymore or that your financial life will no longer allow for any spontaneity.

I know people who use budgets and those who don't. The ones who do say it helps keep things in balance. Those who don't admit to feeling anxious about their "throw caution to the wind" approach.

Talk with someone who lives on a budget and let them tell you how it feels. Pay particular attention to how many people you have to ask before someone says, "Yes, I budget." For most, the budget fits on one page. For others, a more in-depth analysis may be required.

The main goal of a budget is to help you live within your means and address necessary short- and long-term financial goals. It also helps you check to see if your money habits and your values are in alignment. Remember, misalignment can happen rapidly.

When Is It Not Okay to Use a Credit Card?

Nothing is so good as it seems beforehand.
    —George Eliot (Marian Evans Cross) (1819–1880)[11]

Susan, a 33-year-old budget believer, knows exactly when she can and cannot use a credit card. She knows her limits. For example, each month she allots a certain amount for entertainment. If she doesn't have the cash, she doesn't go out unless it's a free activity.

Although some people are born with that discipline, I believe the majority discover it through trial and error. That's not a bad thing, as long as you learn from your mistake of spending more than you earn. Credit card companies make billions of dollars each year off of people who have yet to answer this question.

To assess your situation, try this simple exercise on

158

needs versus wants. Take your last three credit card statements and mark an "N" beside each purchase that was truly
a need: groceries, clothing (not designer labels), and shelter.
Mark a "W" for wants beside all other purchases. Add up the
totals for each letter, and compare the difference. If you
carry a balance on your card, you're probably purchasing too
many wants. Reevaluate purchase decisions to help yourself
establish boundaries for when it is not okay to use your card.

What Factors Should and Should Not Influence Your Purchasing Decisions?

*We are what we consume. If we look deeply into the items
that we consume every day, we will come to know our own
nature very well.*
—Thich Nhat Hanh, Zen Buddhist monk (b. 1926)[12]

Make two lists, one for the factors that should influence your
purchasing decisions and one for the factors that shouldn't.
I'll suggest a few to get you started: peer pressure, kid pressure,
advertising, brand names, your parents, how much you make,
how much you owe, how much you save, how much you
share. You can take it from here. Your answers to other questions might suggest additional factors. The ultimate payoff
comes in affirming or establishing your financial boundaries.

How Can You Be a Good Financial Role Model for Your Child?

*Train children in the right way, and when old they will not
stray.*
—Proverbs 22:6[13]

In every survey I have seen, parents are the runaway leader
at determining how and why their children share, save,

and spend money. I have witnessed many families where children make excellent financial decisions because their parents took the time to show them—how to make good spending decisions; why it's important to save for a goal; why sharing with charities is part of their financial value system.

So often, what you deem important is what your child will do. If you abdicate your role, the three-headed monster will step in and fill the void. Advertisers thrive on inattentive parents. You do not have to be a Wall Street wizard to play this part. You do need a basic grasp of your own financial plan. More important, you need to be alert to the fact that your actions and conversations around all things financial speak volumes to your child.

How Often Should You Review Your Financial Habits?

There is nothing harder than the softness of indifference.
—Juan Montalvo, Latin American philosopher
(1832–1889)[14]

Your answer probably depends on how comfortable you are with your current financial boundaries. If they are well established and you have good balance and rhythm to your financial actions, a couple of times a year might be adequate. If all of this is new and you are having money trouble, a weekly review may be appropriate. Remember, procrastination only contributes to the festering anxiety of imbalanced financial habits.

Decide what is right for you, and stick with your decision. As you do a review, ask whether your financial habits help you live within your means and meet your short- and long-term goals. Periodically, repeat the Financial Habits Checkup. If your score drops, you're making progress!

How Often Should You Discuss Your Financial Values with Your Child?

From the moment of his birth the customs into which [an individual] is born shape his experience and behavior. By the time he can talk, he is the little creature of his culture.
—Ruth Fulton Benedict, American
anthropologist (1887–1948)[15]

The frequency of your discussions depends on the financial personality of your child. If your child exhibits a balanced approach to money, occasional talks might do the job. If your child spends quickly or often kicks into nag mode, your conversations will be more frequent.

Some parents pick out a specific time—like dinner or a family meeting—to discuss their values. Others look for teachable moments, like going to the bank, writing out a check to a charity, or a regular trip to the grocery store. When I was a child, my parents used a combination of the two. Their decision to discuss financial values frequently played a significant role in how I use money today.

The younger, the better for these talks, but it's never too late to start. I've seen people in their 80s finally tell their adult children why they drafted their will as they did. In the end, words are important but only if you consistently demonstrate those ideas in your actions.

What Steps Can You Take to Reduce Your Financial Anxiety?

If we compare the rich with the poor, it often seems that those with nothing are, in fact, the least anxious, although they are plagued with physical pain and suffering. The rich are so caught up in the idea of acquiring still more that they make no room for anything else in their lives [so] they actually lose the dream of happiness.

—The Dalai Lama[16]

161

It is normal to have guilt pangs over things you have or have not done. But don't let that immobilize you. Use your new awareness as a springboard to align your financial behavior with your values. Make this a step forward for you and your child. Consider these possible steps:

- Incorporate your new insights when you create your short- and long-term financial goals, including a budget.
- Seek the guidance of a professional financial adviser. Why? Time and accountability. Addressing financial matters often falls to the bottom of the priority list, especially if no one is around to help you stay on track. If the adviser dismisses the importance of linking financial decisions with your values, consider finding another adviser.

Financial Habits versus Financial Values

The moment of truth is upon us. It's time to compare your answers from the Financial Habits Checkup against those from the Financial Values Reflection. Have you strayed from the route you want to follow? Is your use of money consistent with your values? Don't be surprised if you need to adjust your financial habits to match your financial values.

Refer to your score on the checkup to get a better idea of the degree of conflict between your habits and your values. The better your score, the less likely there will be a problem. But in areas where there is noticeable conflict, consider addressing that issue with a simple plan to improve congruity.

For example, you may have answered yes to the question "Do you lose sleep worrying about money?" But if you took the time to answer the 15 Financial Values questions, you may have already identified ways to reduce your financial anxiety—saving for retirement, more responsible use of your credit card, establishing an emergency fund, and saving for major purchases. All these actions can have a direct impact on how well you sleep.

By establishing written financial priorities you can leverage your answers from the Financial Values questions into positive solutions. Some steps may require the help of a professional adviser, be it financial, legal, or tax. While it's important to move forward, be careful not to burden yourself with wholesale changes today.

Aligning your habits with your values is a lifelong process. Few people have perfect alignment at any one time. Be open to reviewing, refining, and celebrating small successes along the way.

Given the reality of America's commercialization, it is vital to have a personal financial philosophy to guide your decision-making. Without one, you can become easy prey, oftentimes unknowingly, of marketers. Without a financial philosophy, you will be overmatched when trying to establish healthy financial boundaries for your children.

I believe a successful financial philosophy incorporates four factors:

1. **Customization.** Your philosophy must be tailored to your personal situation.

2. **Time.** You need to invest your time—not just your money—to examine what is important to you and then determine how to live in a way that is consistent with your values.

3. **Help.** Since most people haven't received much guidance on financial matters, it's important to seek out resources, such as a financial adviser, that can help you develop a successful approach.

4. Balance. Consider adopting a financial philosophy that incorporates a balance of sharing, saving, and spending. The simplicity of the approach will be your greatest ally. The next chapter defines this concept further.

Your financial philosophy takes shape with refined habits, new priorities, and refocused values, all pointing toward a balanced outlook for your future. Some may call this approach idealistic. I call it realistic. Once you get accustomed to living your philosophy, your kids are sure to follow. If you ever sense the three-headed monster trespassing on your financial values, revisit this chapter for a refresher.

Those that master the art of balanced financial values always have a philosophy guiding their decision process. From the people I know, a strong philosophy is never complicated, but it is ever present.

In your lifetime, you will make hundreds of thousands of financial decisions that add up to millions of dollars. Some will be momentous, others simple and routine. Embrace the opportunity those decisions present. Let your outlook and approach shine through in shaping the financial values of your child.

Chapter TEN

A Balanced Life—
Sharing, Saving, Spending

Ted and Diane, two insightful middle-class parents, recognized a critical change in their 5-year-old son, Andrew. "Soon after he entered kindergarten, he seemed to have a greater interest in money and what it could do for him," said Ted. Their big tip-off came when Andrew kicked into "I want" mode.

For many, that behavior might not seem out of the ordinary. After all, what normal 5-year-old doesn't lob a few requests at Mom or Dad to test the waters? But Ted and Diane saw the behavior change as a warning sign. "His persistence in asking for things was quite noticeable," Ted said. "So we followed our instinct to start teaching him about money."

Whatever your child's age, unless you're ready for it, talking and teaching about money can be difficult. Many struggle to find the right approach. One woman told me how frustrating the experience had been because she rarely saw results. However, she admitted to not always following through and realized she may have been part of the problem.

She's not alone, but at least she had identified the single

greatest barrier to success. Even the best-laid plan can derail without consistent follow-through. In the families with whom I've worked, two issues are to blame for this derailment: Either families haven't fully committed to a specific system, or the system is too complicated or too time-consuming.

Ted and Diane sensed this could be a problem. Enter Sharing-Saving-Spending. "We wanted to introduce an allowance to our son but in a way that engaged his curiosity and reinforced important values," said Diane. They divided Andrew's allowance into three equal parts: one-third for sharing, one-third for saving, and one-third for spending. Andrew's allowance started at 75 cents, with a quarter for each third. Six years later, the family still uses the same method, and Andrew's younger brother participates as well.

"Our primary goal has always been to teach responsible money management. This approach works because it is easy to implement and has helped us set important financial boundaries," said Diane. Both Ted and Diane agree they have virtually eliminated the "I wants" because most of the smaller purchasing decisions now rest with the kids.

Having a balanced approach to financial matters means aligning your values with how you use your money. It means recognizing the opportunities and responsibilities that are part of sound money management. It also means recognizing the interdependent nature of both your own internal and the external needs of others. Adopting this approach ensures that you and your children consciously address present and future financial issues while building up immunity to unhealthy spontaneous consumption.

The beauty of Sharing-Saving-Spending is its simplicity. Not only does it give you the necessary structure, but it also creates unique and varied learning opportunities. You will see that come to life in examples that follow. But first let me give you an overview of the approach and how it can bring balance to your child's use of money.

Sharing

You may be wondering: Why lead with sharing? Sharing comes first because it offers the most effective counter-rhythm for all the messages on spending. Most parents disdain the thought of raising a selfish child. But the overwhelming majority of messages young people receive about money tell them to spend it as soon as they get it and, more specifically, to spend it on their wants. Emphasizing sharing first reminds kids to look around and develop sensitivity to the needs of others. Doing so counters the relentless message that "stuff" makes the person.

Saving

Saving is defined in broad terms to encompass all short- and long-term goals on your child's radar screen. They could include money for a trip; saving to buy something small like a book or big like a car; and investing long-term for something like college. By building routine into their saving process, you reinforce the concept of deferred gratification. Again, rarely do young people hear messages espousing the value of saving. Instead, it's always about getting something today. As you read in earlier chapters, Americans don't do well at deferred gratification. Emphasizing saving ahead of spending is a helpful and necessary reminder to address short- and long-term goals. Getting into the habit of saving early will serve your child well for a lifetime.

Spending

In too many instances, spending overwhelms the ability to share or save. The single greatest barrier to achieving financial balance, spending deserves the metaphors of runaway trains and cars without brakes. If you are not careful, kids

How Much Do You Share, Save, and Spend?

	Example		You	
	$	%	$	%
Take-home pay	50,000	100	_____	_____
Sharing	2,000	4	_____	_____
Saving	4,000	8	_____	_____
Spending	44,000	88	_____	_____

Take-home pay: If all your income was reported on a W-2 wage and tax statement, subtract the amounts you paid for federal income tax, Social Security (FICA), Medicare, state income tax, and local income tax from the amount you received in wages, tips, and other compensation. If you are self-employed, use your most recent tax forms and year-end accounting report to calculate a comparable number.

Sharing: If you itemized deductions on your federal income taxes, use the amount from Line 18 on your Schedule A. Otherwise, add all your cash donations to charitable organizations plus the value of other donations, such as food and clothing, plus the cost of transportation for all volunteer activities.

Saving: Add the amounts you put into retirement accounts, investments, and savings accounts. Year-end statements from banks and brokerage firms help pinpoint those figures.

Spending: Subtract the amounts for sharing and saving from your take-home pay to determine your amount for spending.

If you can't document these figures, estimate to the best of your ability.

To convert the dollar amounts to a percentage, divide the amount for sharing by the amount for take-home pay, then multiply by 100. Repeat for saving and for spending.

can go in the wrong direction at an early age, and reversing course can be difficult. By placing spending last in the Sharing-Saving-Spending philosophy, you put psychology to work. It's a simple way of reminding you to give attention to sharing and saving before you jump to spending. After all, spending is the easy part. By focusing on sharing and saving, you help your child achieve balance. And by learning the discipline behind sharing and saving, they're likely to gain discipline in their spending. The ability to say, "No, I don't need that," and "No, I can't afford that," will make a difference throughout your child's life.

Walk the Walk

It's been said a thousand times, but I'll offer it once again. To talk the talk, you need to walk the walk. By better understanding the how and why behind your financial decisions, you can teach from a position of strength. Good habits, just like bad habits, can be passed from generation to generation. I learned my approach, no surprise, from my parents, who in turn learned from their parents, and so on.

To assess your current allocation to sharing, saving, and spending, fill in the worksheet on the opposite page. Your most recent federal income tax return and assorted year-end statements will help you figure this quickly.

The breakdown will give you a better idea of how your money tracks with the Sharing-Saving-Spending philosophy. Remember, everything we do with money says something about our values and our priorities. Depending on your outcome, you may want to reevaluate your current allocation. The average American shares approximately 2 percent and saves 3 percent.

Most people have some idea where their money goes, but few have taken the time to assess whether the percentage lines up with their values. The goal: Decide on percentages for sharing, saving, and spending, then work toward the desired outcome. At the very least, you will assess how you currently spend money. And at the very most, I hope you will experience great joy and satisfaction from aligning your financial decisions with your values.

The Secret to Allowance

Tracy and Bruce, she a non-profit executive and he an engineer, had dabbled in a "fee for service" allowance, trading money for chores. But they didn't like the concept of paying their kids to be a member of the family. The final straw was when they had a dinner party and the boys asked the guests for tips to bus their dishes. Soon after, the light bulb went on when they read in a newspaper article some reasons for disconnecting allowances from chores.

Too often I see parents give up on allowance because they can't keep track of all the jobs or don't want the tension of having to debate the quality of the job. After all, what are you going to do if your child says, "I'm skipping all my jobs this week because I don't need the money"? Teaching your kids about money should not necessitate high-blood-pressure medication.

The goal of an allowance should be to teach your kids how to manage money. My advice: Use allowance to transfer financial responsibility and accountability to your child and to instill the Sharing-Saving-Spending financial philosophy.

Tracy and Bruce said this approach made all the difference in the world in teaching their boys about money. "We wanted Jason and Peter to learn a few simple lessons: When it comes to money, be responsible. There's more to money than spending. You will value your financial decisions more if you make them," Tracy said. I totally agree.

Many people ask me for the ideal age to start an allowance. My suggestion? As soon as the child says "I want," which is usually by age 5.

After talking with many parents who have success with allowances, three common themes emerged. First is *time*. They use the weekly allowance distribution as a reminder to spend time talking with their kids about money. Second is *patience*. They realize that instilling healthy financial habits doesn't happen overnight, so they have committed to staying the course for the long haul. Third is *consistency*. They understand that a successful system is dependent on consistent behavior both in allowance distribution and in how they role model healthy money habits.

If your child is 13 or younger, try the three-jar system. Label one Sharing, one Saving, and one Spending. I'll talk about more specific ideas for each word in Chapters 11, 12, and 13. When you pay the allowance, let your child put the proper amount into each jar. The physical action will be a powerful reinforcer for the share, save, spend concept. Some parents like Doug will link certain behaviors and actions to the allowance. "While I don't connect their allowance to chores, I will remove some of the money from their spend jar if they misbehave," said Doug. So far, so good, says Doug.

If your child is 14 or older, you can use the same approach, but consider establishing a checking account and a savings account for your child as the primary tools for managing money. The timing should coordinate well with your child's first job. Although some kids learn how to manage a checkbook in school, you may want to offer initial guidance. As his or her income climbs, you may need to have more conversations on how your child allocates the money.

Have your kids keep track of each jar with a simple logbook. Divide each page into three columns (see Table 10.1) to make it easy to add or subtract from each category. If you have a computer, you may want to use a simple spreadsheet. Bottom line, use whatever system will help your children track what they do with their money so they can see patterns emerge over time.

Tracy and Bruce decided to set a weekly allowance for their boys at $1 per year of the child's age. And they required that the allowance be split three ways for sharing, saving, and spending.

The parents have been delighted with the results. The nag factor is gone. Savings are up and more goal-oriented. Sharing is up and more structured.

Table 10.1 Simple Logbook Example

Sharing	Saving	Spending

Chapter ELEVEN

A Balanced Life—Sharing

I credit a particular event when I was very young for getting me hooked on sharing. The year was 1971 and I was six years old. My parents ran a church camp outside of Chetek, Wisconsin. Each summer, a different musical missionary group would come to camp and share their message. For reasons I can't explain, that year was different. After the group's performance, they talked about their upcoming trip overseas and asked people in the audience to share what they could to help offset the cost for travel and supplies. I decided I wanted to participate but didn't have any money with me.

So I climbed on my bike, rode home, reached into my money jar and pulled out $15, which was all the money I had. Back on the bike, I headed to camp and searched out the leader of the group. I wasn't sure how he would react because I didn't think it would be much help. I couldn't have been more wrong.

He squatted down to my level, put out his hand and shook mine while looking me right in the eye and said, "Thank you." For the next five minutes or so, he talked with me about what a great thing I had done. He told me how my contribution would help buy school supplies for a child my age in the country they were visiting. In all, he must have thanked me at least ten times. Later that evening, my parents commented on how proud they were of my decision to help out. I'm now 38, and I remember that day like it was yesterday.

Moral of the story: *Never underestimate the impact of a generous act on a young person.* The feeling I had after making the decision to share my money was fantastic. And it was greatly enhanced when affirmed by the group's leader and my parents. Looking back, that was one experience that began to shape my financial values. I didn't realize it at the time, and I'm sure my parents didn't either, but today the impact of that one event seems abundantly clear.

We teach young children that sharing is good when it comes to toys, games, and playing with their friends, yet sharing is virtually absent when teaching kids about money. Are we missing a golden opportunity to shape their financial values? Absolutely! According to a Yankelovich Survey for Lutheran Brotherhood, nearly 70 percent of teens think it is important to give money to charities or people who need it. And an impressive 62 percent have followed through and shared their money. All they lack is a little encouragement and reinforcement.

Instilling the value of sharing might be one of the most beneficial things you can do for your child. Sharing gives children a sense of purpose and belonging in a world that needs their talent and ideas. I also think they better understand their role in society when they take the time to look around and see the needs of the world. Sharing helps transfer important values of giving back money and time to a cause or organization they may be passionate about. And by being more aware, maybe they'll identify an issue that needs attention and rally others to offer a hand.

Where Are the Sharing Messages?

By their very nature, young people are generous. They are more optimistic and idealistic than most adults. Nearly 40 percent of kids age 8 to 17 said they dream about helping other people in the future, according to the 2000 Roper Youth Report. For further proof, talk with recent college graduates. Often, they have an air that suggests "I can change the world."

But what is society doing to reinforce their innate desire to be generous? Whether it's young children or teens, they seldom hear messages encouraging them to share—especially when it comes to money.

I asked a roomful of 200 New York City middle-school students and their parents a question that proved surprisingly difficult: How many commercials or advertisements have you seen encouraging you to share? And, if you have, can you name any? Judging by their reaction, you would have thought I asked them to solve an advanced calculus problem in their heads.

After staring blankly for a few moments, someone shouted, "The United Way commercials during NFL games." Eventually, someone mentioned another commercial for feeding people overseas, but overall they were stumped. I could tell that, until I asked the question, most of the kids and parents had never given it any thought.

When teaching a financial philosophy of sharing first, parents find little reinforcement for their effort. There will be days when you feel as though you're swimming against the current. It's you versus Madison Avenue.

The people I have met who are diligent in teaching sharing have a wonderfully grounded sense of financial balance. For them, it's not a question of "can I afford to give money and time away"; rather it's a need to look beyond themselves and respond to the needs of the world.

Lessons on Sharing

In the rest of this chapter, I outline creative ways to help you teach sharing habits to your child. As with all the suggestions, I encourage you to choose the exercise that works for you. My hope is that some of the ideas will be springboards for creating teachable moments for you and your children.

Teach by Example

Place a "sharing jar" in a prominent place, like the kitchen table, and fill it with your loose change. When it gets full, have your child add up the total. Then decide as a family how you are going to share it. The jar serves as a great visual reminder to have frequent sharing conversations.

Set Expectations

Setting expectations for sharing can be helpful if the concept of sharing is new to your family or if you want to reinforce how serious you are about making charitable donations. Because kids receive very few messages to share, setting an expectation (whether a dollar amount or a percentage) is an important first step in making sharing part of your family's financial habits.

Consider the story of Devon from Martin County, Florida. When she was 6, her dad taught her to calculate 10 percent of her money by moving the decimal point over one place. "I would take 10 percent of my money out of my savings and put it aside to help somebody in need," said Devon.

Soon, she started to take her charity money to the grocery store to buy a few cans of cat and dog food and then drop them off at the Humane Society. "I would always look forward to charity day," she said. Her dad taught her other percentages, like 20 percent and 30 percent, and each time she increased her giving. To further encourage Devon, her parents decided to match every dollar she set aside for charity.

Soon she was getting letters from charities, asking her to help them, too. "Every month or so, I would sit down with my dad and go through all of the letters that had come to decide which ones I wanted to send some money to," Devon said. And help she did!

In 2000 she raised $1300 for the American Heart Association and was recognized as the Top Junior Fund Raiser. In 2001, she decided to dedicate her tenth birthday to the local Humane Society. "I spent three months collecting pet supplies and money to help build a new animal shelter in Palm City," said Devon. In all, she collected over two tons of pet food and supplies, as well as $3500 for the building fund.

In 2002 she was at it again. "I had heard our local shelter for abused and neglected kids needed new beds, so I decided to dedicate my eleventh birthday to them." Her goal was $8000. She raised $52,000. Most recently, Sears named her National Kid's Hero and awarded her $2100 to share with the charity of her choice. Her plans for the future: "I hope to be a Junior Adoption Specialist at the animal shelter when I'm old enough (next year). They help people who are looking for a pet find the right one. That way I can help animals who don't have a home."

Devon is a unique individual. But look at what happens when you combine encouraging parents with organizations that take young people seriously. Every child is capable of sharing time, sharing talent, and sharing money. I like to think of that as sharing cubed.

Invite Relatives to Promote Sharing

Bill and I were riding in a car outside of Philadelphia when he shared a fantastic idea that his in-laws had adopted. Bill, in his mid-40s and speaking with lots of enthusiasm, said his in-laws are charitable people and had been searching for a way to pass on that value to their grandkids.

After a little brainstorming, they devised a plan. In addition to the traditional gift-giving they did for holidays and birthdays, they added a twist. They would write out a check with everything filled in except the line following "pay to the order of." There was only one rule the grandkids had to follow in filling out the check: The money had to be shared with a charitable organization.

Bill said the checks generate lots of great conversation in their house. "It is a terrifically simple concept, but it gives their grandparents a chance to share more than just material things. Kathryn, our youngest daughter, really thinks hard before she makes that final decision," he said. Bill also appreciates having other people discuss the value of sharing with their kids. "When it comes to money, we try hard to set good boundaries for our kids. But that added reinforcement has been very helpful," he said.

Calling all grandparents, aunts, uncles and, yes, even parents! Try giving a sharing check just once. If you do, you'll be hooked. I have done it for several years with nieces and nephews. Once I even received an unexpected thank you note from my nephew's junior high band director. He shared his check with the music program to help buy new band equipment.

How great would it be if sharing checks became a regular part of birthdays and holidays? It works great with adults, too. So the next time you think, "I have no idea what to buy this person," think of a "share check."

Shift Perspective During Consumer-Oriented Events

On those occasions that can bring out selfish tendencies, shift your child's attention to those in need:

- **Birthdays:** Does your child have adequate amounts of "stuff?" If you throw a party, consider taking a different path this year. On the invitations, ask for a donation to a child-oriented charity, such as Make a Wish Foundation, instead of gifts. You will be the talk of the neighborhood and revered by parents who quietly wonder when all the unnecessary gift-giving will end. Consider it a variation on the "share check."

- **Back-to-School Shopping:** To defuse a potentially unpleasant experience and minimize the nag factor, try this approach. Tell your child you are adding something new to the shopping list—an article of clothing or school supplies for a child who can't afford them. And make it clear that you want your child's help in picking it out. Most school districts welcome donations. If yours does not, talk to a local religious organization or United Way office. This will introduce a whole new element to the shopping experience.

- **Holiday Season:** Is your child looking to buy a gift for someone who has everything? Help your child think of a charitable cause the recipient supports, and then make a donation in that person's honor.

- **Time:** Our society is conditioned that when time with your children is running short, the easy fallback is to buy them something as a substitute. This can be true for grandparents and other family members as well. As mentioned earlier in the book, most young people would prefer our time over material gifts. So whether you're a parent, grandparent, aunt, or uncle, if you feel the urge to swap time with a gift, revisit your schedule to see whether you could spend time doing something together. And when and where it's appropriate, let them know who taught you about sharing. Intergenerational discussions can be a powerful teaching tool.

Encourage Creativity

After speaking at a workshop in Arizona, I met a retired woman who recalled her most memorable birthday present with such clarity you might have thought it happened last month. One week before her forty-fourth birthday, her 14-year-old son was noticeably excited. Understand, few 14-year-old boys get excited for their mom's birthday. But this year was different. His excitement bubbled over from the present he had purchased—a goat.

He had learned that, if he shared a certain dollar amount, a hunger-relief organization such as Heifer International could buy a goat for a drought-stricken village overseas. Her son wanted to help, and he knew his mother was passionate about this cause. So, rather than buying her the typical birthday present she might soon forget, he bought her a goat. "It was and still is the most memorable gift anyone has ever given me. It touched me deeply to know my son understood how important this issue was for me," she said. And so, with a little creativity, the son turned another birthday celebration into a lifelong memory.

Sharing is good for the soul. It stretches us to do creative things we might never have embraced. That's the great thing with young people. Give them a creative inch, and they'll likely stretch it a mile. Just imagine how many creative sharing opportunities are waiting to be discovered by your child.

Link Sharing with Serving

Remember, sharing is about more than just money. If you give to a local charity, think about volunteering together as a family. Try to match your child's talents with an organization. If your son is an artist and a local nursing home has an art class, he could share his skills with the residents. There is nothing like a hands-on experience to reinforce the idea of sharing. It also serves as a much-needed counter-rhythm to the onslaught of consumer messages.

Service learning, the academic version of sharing time and talent, is growing in popularity at U.S. colleges and universities. By combining academic learning with a volunteer activity, schools raise their students' awareness of social issues. According to recent studies, the impact on the students has been impressive.

Researchers at UCLA discovered that young people who participate in service learning maintained their grade point average, and nearly 30 percent improved their GPA. Students also noted a heightened public awareness as well as knowledge and acceptance of different races and cultures. So successful is this approach that many colleges and universities now incorporate it into their curriculum.

Be Patient

For Leslee and Jim, a couple that has worked hard to instill lessons of financial balance and responsibility, a check in the amount of $24.70 was cause to celebrate. Leslee, the mother of 17-year-old Hans, tells a touching story of how Jim discovered the sharing message had really taken root.

One Sunday, Jim had the job of counting the offering for their medium-sized church. What made Jim stop in his tracks was a check for $24.70. Turns out it was from his son, Hans, who holds a part-time job. Immediately, Jim knew the reason for the odd dollar amount. It was exactly 10 percent of Hans' paycheck.

"When Jim came home and told me what had happened, I was really moved," said Leslee. She said they work hard to instill the value of sharing with their two boys but weren't sure how much the message had sunk in. "It's at times like this that you feel a real sense of accomplishment," she said. "To see that he had taken the message of sharing so literally was really touching."

Patience is a virtue. Teaching lessons on money, especially sharing, requires lots of patience. But when you sprinkle in a bit of persistence, your efforts can make a huge difference. What you teach today will likely be repeated for years in the future.

Start Today

Implementing one of these ideas can be instantaneous. Lynne, who works in the development office at St. Olaf College, attended a meeting where I discussed the Sharing-Saving-Spending philosophy and easily adopted this approach with Michael, her 13-year-old son.

"The next day Michael and I established his 'give-back fund.' Together we decided that anytime he received money, whether it was from walking the neighbor's dog or from his grandparents, some portion—up to 10 percent—would go into the fund," she said. When enough money accumulates, he gives it away. His current charity of choice is the school library.

We Need More Mosquitoes

Instilling the joy of sharing in young people greatly enhances their lives. By establishing this critical first step, you are well on your way to helping your child establish a balanced financial approach. Sharing will always be the best counter-rhythm to the inordinate number of messages to spend. Beyond the issues of money management, you also will help your child develop into a caring and compassionate individual.

The United States is a nation of volunteers and contributors—from the first public libraries and volunteer fire companies begun by Benjamin Franklin to the hundreds who joined Clara Barton's Red Cross in the 1860s. Millions of citizens demonstrate generosity and public spirit each year. To keep that great tradition alive, parents need to invest time and energy into teaching young people a simple financial philosophy, Sharing-Saving-Spending.

An African proverb captures the essence of my point: If you think you are too small to make a difference, try sleeping in a closed room with a mosquito. Consider how 6 year-old Devon caught the sharing bug and wanted to make a difference. Although she had a passion for the Humane Society, it was her parent's encouragement and participation that moved it to another level. They have been with her every step of the way. Whether it was driving her to a fund-raiser or matching some of her donations, their guidance has made a huge difference. So, too, can your participation inspire your child.

Other Resources

The first two sites are great examples of young people combining their creativity with a cause. I share them to inspire your efforts. To honor the leadership of Clara Barton and one of the nation's early charitable organizations, I also recommend visiting the Red Cross site. If you need ideas for a sharing project, try the United Way or Heifer sites.

Change for Change (www.changeforchange.com)
This organization aims to spur philanthropic giving among the college community, no matter how big or small the contribution. They provide a mechanism for college students to make an impact in their local community by allocating funds raised through the collection of loose change and other donations. A simple but powerful concept!

183

Devon's Heal the World Recycling (www.devonshealtheworld. com)

The mission of Devon's "Heal The World" Recycling is to recycle the Earth's natural resources, so that future generations will be able to enjoy the same wonderful world that we enjoy now. Devon uses a significant portion of her business proceeds to support the efforts of local, state, and national organizations who share her passion for healing the world by caring about the environment, animals, and children.

Red Cross (www.redcross.org)

The Red Cross is committed to saving lives and easing suffering. This diverse organization serves humanity and helps provide relief to victims of disaster, both locally and globally. The Red Cross is responsible for half of the nation's blood supply and blood products. In the wake of an earthquake, tornado, flood, fire, hurricane, or other disaster, it provides relief services to communities across the country. The site will help your child understand the varied needs of people around the country and around the world.

United Way of America (www.unitedway.org)

United Way of America is the national organization dedicated to leading the United Way movement with approximately 1400 community-based organizations across the United States. One of its innovative programs is 2-1-1, the national abbreviated dialing code for free access to health and human services information and referral; 2-1-1 helps make a critical connection between individuals and families seeking services or volunteer opportunities and the appropriate community-based organizations and government agencies.

184

Heifer International (www.heifer.org)

Heifer International began in 1930 when a Midwestern farmer, Dan West, ladled out cups of milk to hungry children in civil war–ravaged Spain. As he struggled to keep up with the demand, he discovered that what the children and their families needed was "not a cup, but a cow." He asked his friends back home to each donate a heifer (a young cow that has not borne a calf) so hungry families could feed themselves. In return, they could help another family become self-reliant by passing on to them one of their gift animal's female calves. The idea of giving families a source of food rather than short-term relief caught on and has continued for more than 50 years. As a result, families in 115 countries have enjoyed better health, more income, and the joy of helping others.

Money Talks

- What causes are important to you?
- What causes are important to your child?
- Does your child currently share money or time with an organization or cause?
- Would they benefit from such an experience? And why?
- Do you tell your child why you share your money and/or your time?
- Have you ever done a sharing project as a family?

Chapter TWELVE

A Balanced Life—Saving

Tracy and Bruce, the parents featured in the section on allowance in Chapter 10, had a sense of uneasiness about the future. They repeatedly witnessed irresponsible consumer behavior in their oldest son, Jason. When they projected the behavior into the future, their concern grew exponentially. "We definitely worried about what would happen after he left home. Trying to get him to save for even the smallest thing was challenging. We couldn't imagine how he would handle something bigger, like a car, a house or retirement," said Tracy.

Of the three words in my philosophy, *saving* is the most difficult. While most people know the short- and long-term value of saving money, many stumble on implementing a successful system to accomplish their goals. Tracy and Bruce certainly found that to be the case with Jason.

Then they adopted my Sharing-Saving-Spending philosophy. Giving equal time to each category, they discovered an approach that was straightforward and in sync with their objectives. "Since elevating saving ahead of spending, we have had much more success teaching Jason how to save," Tracy said. "Bruce and I feel better about his ability to save for goals and Jason realizes a sense of accomplishment for sticking to his plan." To their credit, Tracy and Bruce also recognized a need to increase their time and energy devoted to saving conversations.

Many people ask me if there is a "golden nugget"—a bit of wisdom that will make *the* difference in helping their child learn how to save. This is it: A successful outcome depends on frequent conversations on saving and your willingness to be a responsible role model.

If you need motivation to take that important first step, consider what's at stake. The three-headed monster views your child as little more than a lifetime source of consumer purchases. But with discipline, a good system, and words of encouragement, you can counter the marketing machine and help your child realize the value of saving. The best decision Tracy and Bruce made was to alter their approach when it didn't provide adequate results. By facing their fears about Jason's saving habits, they were able to intervene with a good strategy.

No Need for a Finance Degree

Unfortunately, I have witnessed many parents who avoid the subject because they feel unprepared to teach about money. Parents, let me put you at ease. To teach your kids the art of saving, you do not need a degree in finance. In fact, the parents I know who have had success do not count investing as one of their favorite pastimes. Rather, they combine a good system and excellent follow-through with the "learn more as you go" method.

A parent's role in teaching children to save falls into three parts:

1. **Develop a routine to the savings process.** It's best to integrate saving with allowance so that your child learns to save a portion of his or her income. I recommend a weekly allowance and weekly savings because it creates an opportunity to have frequent conversations. Performing the act of saving 52 times a year also helps to ingrain the saving habit. To encourage saving, hundreds of financial books preach the importance of paying yourself first. A routine ensures that will happen.

2. **Teach a basic financial "vocabulary."** By helping your child learn basic savings concepts, you provide a critical head start on becoming financially literate. Your child should know how a savings account works; why the college money is in a mutual fund; how time affects savings; and how unwise spending can impede the ability to save.

3. **Help children experience the joy of reaching a savings goal.** The key is to help kids understand there is a reward for their efforts. You are their primary source of motivation and inspiration to reach the savings goal. Young people need frequent reminders to keep up their efforts at saving. You can be the voice of reason when they are tempted to spend it all today. (More later on short- and long-term goals.)

If you do these three things, you will strengthen your child's financial habits and decisions for years to come. By embracing my Sharing-Saving-Spending philosophy, you elevate saving to its rightful place—ahead of spending.

Where Are the Saving Messages?

Contrary to popular belief, saving is not about chasing the latest investment fad. The art of saving is a combination of time, patience, and disciplined habits. Acknowledging that saving money is a lifelong process will help you establish a more realistic outlook for your child. Saving messages geared toward instant financial success—pick the hot stock and retire wealthy this year—can easily overshadow the patient, methodical approach of saving 10 percent a week, every month, and every year. This is especially true when someone commits to a long-term goal like a house or retirement. By helping your child commit early to a disciplined, goal-oriented approach, you boost his or her potential for long-term success.

In Chapter 11, I described how a group of middle-school kids and parents in New York was stumped when I asked them to name a commercial that encourages them to share their money. Well, I asked the group the same question about saving. No surprise, the response was identical—silence.

Then I asked the young people to huddle up with their parents to brainstorm savings ideas. In five short minutes, they had several suggestions for ways they could infuse saving into their routine. My point: Don't wait for inspiration from an outside source to start conversations on saving money.

Lessons on Saving

Just as sharing means more than money (e.g., volunteering), so, too, does saving mean more than investing. You will recall in Chapter 10 that saving was defined in broad terms to encompass all short- and long-term goals on your child's radar screen. As you generate enthusiasm for saving, try to balance the time you spend on both ends of the spectrum (i.e., savings accounts and mutual funds). Even though the financial markets have been tumultuous lately, there have also been some great teachable moments for people of all ages. Perhaps most important of all, patience is a virtue.

The sooner you take the first step toward instilling the value of saving, the more likely your child will embrace it as part of his or her financial routine. There will be times when it feels like you are teaching one language and society is teaching another. After all, marketing relies on lapses in logic or reality, so stick to your financial philosophy. To improve your success in teaching critical lessons of saving, try the following ideas.

Teach by Example

Again, I suggest a visual aid—a saving jar—in a prominent place in the home to stimulate conversation. Like the sharing jar, a saving jar makes a helpful symbol. Think of it like the string around your finger to have frequent, intentional conversations about money.

Mike, a television producer, said his family uses a savings jar for a state fair fund. With seven kids, he said saving for things like the state fair is important. Each year, the goal is to accumulate enough spare change from their pockets to pay for everyone's admission as well as food and treats. Last year they did so well there was money left over to eat out on the way home. Think of all the lessons from that experience—a shared goal, deferred gratification, a fun experience, and a sense of accomplishment.

Set Expectations

The best way to set savings expectations for your child is to start small with a reachable goal, then build on their knowledge. Even before you put my Sharing-Saving-Spending system in place, talk with your kids about why you think saving is so important. Share a few examples of how you learned or failed to learn to save as a child. If appropriate, use your own story to reinforce why you feel it is important for them to learn about saving. Saving for saving's sake is fine, but connecting it to something meaningful and lasting will help make your point.

For Marian, who grew up at the end of the Depression, teaching her four kids to save was second nature. "We didn't have much money when the kids were real young, but that didn't stop us from setting aside at least 10 percent for the future. Our kids never resisted saving because they saw us sacrifice to save for college and retirement," said Marian. It's not possible to emphasize enough the need to be a role model for saving. The majority of what your child learns will come from observing your actions.

Invite Other Relatives to Help

One of the great values of my grandparents' and parents' generation is their uncanny ability to save money. I have talked with enough of them to know it is more than a fluke. Many of them experienced financial hardship during the Depression. Whether they were an adult or child at the time, the impact changed their lives. A story from a grandparent who remembers how it felt to have little or no food can shape the perspective of a young person.

As a by-product of their saving success, many grandparents want to share the wealth (via gift giving) with their grandkids. As I mentioned in Chapter 6, lots of families wrestle with this problem. My suggestion is to shepherd the money of overzealous gift-buying grandparents and other relatives into a college fund or even a retirement fund.

They don't have to abstain from giving an occasional gift, just redirect the majority of funds into something more lasting. In short, they can be generous and still support your desire to maintain balance. Having a conversation on this topic can save you years of aggravation.

My grandparents, who were of limited means, set aside money each year in an education fund for their grandkids. Because of their generosity I was able to participate in two international study programs while I was in college. Not only were both great experiences, but they piqued my curiosity for learning about other places and cultures.

Discuss Your Goals

Here's a simple suggestion I saw Heidi, a teacher in her early 40s, practice with her three kids. She occasionally shows them her retirement statements (401(k), pension, and mutual funds) and then talks about how much money she saved each year toward her goal. Not only were they shocked at how much it takes to retire, but they developed a new appreciation for long-term financial obligations.

A college fund brings the subject even closer to home. Most young preteens have no idea how much college costs. I have asked hundreds of young kids this question, and they frequently respond with answers ranging from $500 to $50,000 a year. Although I didn't expect them to know exact numbers, it is important for them to understand the size of the goal. Don't hold it over them. Instead, help them understand the cost of an education. To put it in kid-friendly language, I find it helps to compare the price of a new vehicle to one year of college.

Transfer Responsibility

Teaching your child to save and be accountable for his or her decisions is critical to establishing healthy financial boundaries. Part of transferring responsibility is letting young people learn from their mistakes. One father in Seattle shared with me how his 9-year-old son just had to have an ultracool scooter. Those things aren't cheap. His son had saved the money, so the father agreed to let him proceed with the purchase.

In these situations, which happen millions of times a day in the United States, parents know what's coming next. Eventually the thrill wears off, sometimes even the same week. The dejected child often realizes he bought on impulse. As the next step in the grieving process, the child sometimes shifts the blame to someone else. The son in Seattle made his father the target of his disappointment. The son thought dad should replenish the savings account. Dad held fast and let his son learn from the experience. A wise decision.

Turn Wants into Goals

Use goal-setting to counter the "I wants." If your child wants something, let her save for it. It might be small items today, but it will help develop a realistic approach to big-ticket needs and wants like cars, homes, and retirement in the future. Of course, the desire for many wants tends to fade while your child saves, which provides a lesson in itself.

There may be benefits to you as well. As you embrace the opportunity to be a role model, don't be surprised if you have an increased desire to sharpen your savings habits. By assessing your ability to set goals and follow through, you too can improve your prospects for long-term financial success.

Set Short-Term Goals

For most young people, short-term goals are usually earmarked for stuff they want to buy or do. Things like: toys, video games, CDs, going to a movie, eating out with friends, and sports equipment, to name a few.

Even though short-term goals might be for immediate purchases, you can use some of the money to teach your child how a simple savings account works. When either the saving or spending jar reaches $25, head to the bank with your child. It is a great way to build their financial vocabulary and awareness of a financial institution. Don't be surprised if your child says, "You mean a bank will actually pay me to leave my money there?"

Set Long-Term Goals

Rhonda, a self-employed bookkeeper, helped her son, Peter, save for long-term goals early on. As early as age 10, he started talking about owning a car. She used the teachable moment as an opportunity to talk with him about the cost of new cars, used cars, insurance, and upkeep. Rhonda also wanted Peter to understand Mom and Dad weren't going to buy him a car at age 16. But if he saved his money and could pay for two-thirds of it, they would help out with the rest.

"It was a great way to see how serious he was and to help him understand that you have to save for things you want," Rhonda said. Shortly after he turned 17, Peter had saved enough money to pay for his part as well as insurance. "I know he appreciates it more because it was his money," said Rhonda.

For some of you, a long-term goal may present a great opportunity to introduce a mutual fund to your child. Rhonda and her husband used mutual funds to save for college. When the kids received money for birthdays and holidays, Rhonda deposited the funds in the college account. Just as she did with Peter's car goal, she spent time talking about how much college cost and why they were using a mutual fund. Rarely did a financial opportunity pass by that she didn't use it to improve her kids' financial vocabulary.

Not only is it important to establish long-term goals for cars and college, but also spending money for family vacations, a musical instrument and, yes, even emergency funds for that unexpected financial obligation.

Support Good Decision Making

With both short- and long-term saving goals, you'll encounter the all-important need to reinforce your child's good decisions. Rhonda worked hard to encourage Peter's saving goal. Whenever and wherever possible, give positive reinforcement to your child for making a good financial choice. A little encouragement will go a long way in keeping your child motivated as he or she learns how to save. Along the way, your child will discover how tightly saving and spending habits are intertwined.

Provide an Incentive to Save—the Family 401(k)

During one of my workshops near Philadelphia, Lori, the mother of a 7-year-old daughter and a 9-year-old son, said she had great success with something she calls the family 401(k).

Lori wanted to reinforce her kids' decision to save. One day, while reviewing her 401(k) retirement plan, the idea dawned on her to adopt a similar approach with her two kids. Her goal was twofold: First, create a saving activity that was fun and easy to manage. Second, familiarize the kids with an adult concept in anticipation of their first adult job. What a great idea! So many young adults defer enrolling in retirement plans because they have important stuff to buy and retirement seems so far away.

She decided to match 50 cents for every dollar her kids set aside for long-term savings. It wasn't for little trinkets. It was for educational purposes, like computer software, summer learning camps, and college. Lori kept it simple and divided the money into two accounts. If the goal was two years or less, she used a savings account. Anything longer went into a mutual fund.

She also used the family 401(k) to build the kids' financial vocabulary. Once a quarter, they reviewed their statements from the different accounts and compared the results. While much information on the statements is abstract even for most adults, never underestimate the ability of a young person to soak it up. Someday it will click in, and you can take pride in having raised their curiosity early on. Although

195

your specific purpose might differ from Lori's, the family 401(k) is worth trying.

Be Patient

Some parents believe they have a born spender and nothing they can do will change that. I refer you back to Jason, the son of Tracy and Bruce from the beginning of the chapter. Since his parents adopted a new approach to allowances, Jason's money management skills have greatly improved. It didn't happen overnight. "Our youngest son, Peter, picked up the concept right away, but Jason needed a little more time," Tracy said.

Now that the system has taken root, Jason saves money to buy his friends birthday presents and he negotiated with his brother Peter to pool their money to buy a video game console. Helping young people adopt good saving habits takes time. If you approach it with an open mind and build their skills a little at a time, you will see results.

Start Today

Understanding how money grows at different rates of return is an important concept for your kids. Even more important, help your children understand how time affects their investment. Too many times I have witnessed young adults in their 20s and early 30s who have yet to develop the discipline to save for a goal. This can prove costly on long-term needs like saving for a house or retirement.

In the fall of 2001 I led a workshop, "Your Money, Your Future: Take Control," on college campuses to help students understand the critical role money plays in their lives. A segment on the importance of saving for the future created an "Aha!" moment for the students. I used the following example to reinforce the need to start saving today:

Two hypothetical people graduated from college and landed good jobs with excellent benefits. Although both recognized the need to save for retirement, they took decidedly different paths. Eric put off saving until age 45, when he decided to save $700 a year for 20 years while earning a 6 percent rate of return. By the time Eric reached age 65, the investment was worth approximately $25,000.

Jessica decided to make a few sacrifices at age 25 and save the same $700 a year for 20 years at 6 percent interest. At age 45, Jessica took ill and could no longer continue to invest. Upon reaching age 65, the investment was worth approximately $83,000—more than three times the amount in Eric's account.

The moral of the story: Save early and save often. Investment returns move up and down, but time never wavers in helping you reach important financial goals. This example helped the college students learn the value of compounding.

A Skill for Life

Tracy and Bruce found that, by transferring appropriate amounts of financial responsibility to their son, he began to take the long view on financial decisions. "Before we switched our approach, Jason was losing money, borrowing from his brother and impulse buying. Today, he takes full responsibility for his financial decisions," Tracy said.

As with other life skills, the day will come when you say, "What will be, will be." How much better will you feel knowing you contributed to your child's financial well-being? Regardless of your child's age, start today. I'm a firm believer that anyone can change his or her behavior as long as the teacher believes in the message. Embrace the opportunity. Both you and your child will benefit for years to come. Remember, good habits are hard to break.

Other Resources

I have included three sites that will be helpful in building you and your child's financial vocabulary. While each site focuses on more than saving money, they do offer good suggestions for helping everybody in the family reach their savings goals.

Choose to Save (www.choosetosave.org)

This public education program promotes the idea that saving today is vital to a secure financial future. They also provide Internet tools to help consumers plan all aspects of their financial security, which includes the award-winning *Ballpark Estimate Retirement Planning Worksheet* to estimate how much you need to save for retirement. Choose to Save also has over 100 online financial calculators to help you with a wide array of financial planning issues including credit, home mortgage, and budgeting.

Right on the Money! (www.rightonthemoney.org)

Right on the Money! is a personal finance television show that helps people solve their own money problems and provides tools to help build their financial futures. Now in its fourth season, the half-hour weekly series is produced by TPT/Twin Cities Public Television, and is hosted by award-winning journalist and financial expert Chris Farrell. The site lists upcoming shows and presents the latest ideas about finance.

Each episode takes viewers on a journey through the world of personal finance with great money tips and advice along the way. The series focuses on families with real-life financial situations. Chris and company take you step-by-step through a problem in every episode and, with a team of leading financial experts, identify the guest family's best money options. It's an excellent show for the whole family.

Sound Money (www.soundmoney.org)

Whether you're living paycheck to paycheck or living on your investment income, Sound Money has information you can use to improve your financial situation. The weekly public radio program, which again features Chris Farrell, contains several interviews with special guests who address a wide variety of topics for individual investors and consumers. The site also offers recommendations on helpful books, tools, and other web sites.

Money Talks

- Why are you teaching your child to save?
- Ask your child what are some ways they can save their money?
- Ask your child if they know how you save money, and for what.
- How frequently (i.e., weekly, monthly) do you talk about saving?
- Do you know someone who sets a good example in how they save their money?
- Have you adopted a system for teaching the art of saving money?
- If you are using an allowance, is it working?
- Was there a savings goal that your child accomplished recently?
- If yes, did you celebrate their achievement?

Chapter THIRTEEN

A Balanced Life—Spending

S helly loves to shop. Rarely a week goes by that she isn't wandering the local mall looking for that special something to satisfy her urge to buy. It doesn't take much—a new shirt, some makeup, or a CD. There's one little problem. Shelly is only 14, and she shadows the movements of her mother.

Ever since she can remember, Shelly and her mom have made the weekly trip to the mall. When Mom buys, Shelly buys. Mom exclaims how great the new jeans look on Shelly, and Shelly roots for Mom to buy the "really cool" necklace. Shelly knows she has a great time shopping with her mom. However, she doesn't know that her mom carries a load of credit card debt.

Millions of young children witness their parents' daily consumer decisions from the seat of a grocery cart or a stroller in a mall. One by one, various exchanges begin to shape the perspective of the child. Collectively, they form the foundation for the child's emerging financial values. As with other learned behaviors, when the child begins to make her own consumer decisions, parental impressions play a key role.

My, How Times Have Changed

I believe that learning how to spend is more complicated and abstract today than at any time in our history. As recently as 30 years ago, the majority of adults bought with cash. And that's what a child would have witnessed. It was either cash pulled from a wallet or a check written from a bank account. Even for a 5-year-old the exchange of cash for a product is pretty straightforward.

While few people may resemble the behavior of Shelly's mom, note the common factors. Consider what your child might be thinking the next time you use your credit card or stop for cash at the ATM. You perpetuate what you model. Unless you take a few minutes to demystify the experience for your child, the transaction infuses a dose of unreality. If your child never sees you pay the bill for those "plastic purchases" or deduct from your account after "magically" withdrawing money, he probably does not understand how the loop closes.

For proof, look no farther than the consumer debt crisis of many college students. Even though most have at least two credit cards, they do not understand what Annual Percentage Rate (APR) means. Nor do they understand that banks offer the minimum-payment option as a way to prolong debt. Working part-time and charging trips, meals, clothes, and other discretionary purchases, they represent an emerging class of "nouveau poor" in the United States.

Since the time they were babies, they have been duped into thinking "stuff" makes the "person." Now on the brink of adulthood, they consider small mountains of debt as normal. Their habits weren't formed in college; they took shape years before as they observed others around them—especially parents.

Spending comes last in the Sharing-Saving-Spending philosophy because virtually every message and impression encourages a young person to spend early and spend often. In Chapter 4, The Teen Commandments, I discussed how attitudes that stimulate spending by young people start to develop at a young age. The Sharing-Saving-Spending philosophy provides levelheaded guidance amid the consumer frenzy. It helps you train your child to be a grounded, savvy spender.

In my years of interacting with people about money, I have never met anyone who follows this philosophy and has spending trouble. Not one. Whether they are 70 or 27 years old, of wealthy or modest means, they all share a commitment to put spending in its proper perspective.

Lessons on Spending

Following are several suggestions to help you establish a foundation for spending. These ideas are straightforward and ready for immediate implementation.

Teach by Example

Let me reiterate the importance of parental role modeling. Shelly's mom, the woman at the beginning of the chapter, may not be the best consumer role model, but on a continuum of tightwad to spendthrift, the margin of error is significant. With the preponderance of consumer temptations, living within your means can challenge even the most disciplined spender. In teaching your child about money, few issues are as critical as your own regular consumer decisions.

The challenge and the opportunity lie in periodically reviewing where you stand. In Chapter 9, Your Money, Your Values, I asked you to assess your financial habits and suggested that you review the entries in your checkbook and credit card receipts for the last six months. Take a closer look at that information to determine how much you spend in assorted categories. If you balance your checkbook with computer software, you can quickly create a report. You can do the same thing on paper, although you might want to review just two or three months at a time.

Consider how much you spent on clothing, food, entertainment, and travel during the past months. In the food category, how much was for groceries, and how much was for dining out? For example, the average U.S. family spends roughly half of its food dollars on dining out. How do you feel about the amounts in each category? In what areas have you spent more than you intended? Knowing how you spent money in the past makes you more sensitive to your own spending going forward.

In the coming weeks, challenge yourself to say no to your own wants and to opt for less expensive options. After one or two months, total your spending in the four categories for the period. How has the average per month changed? Are your financial habits in better alignment with your financial values? Give yourself another Financial Habits Checkup from Chapter 9. Has your score improved? If you change your spending habits, you send a message to your child through your actions and create opportunities to discuss your new decisions.

Set Expectations

While spending is a necessary part of existence, establishing expectations for how your child makes decisions will help build important boundaries. Expectations for reasonable spending vary from family to family. However, some common variables will come into play: the child's age; the child's ability to grasp money concepts; off-limits purchases (such as violent video games or inappropriate clothing); if and how allowance is used; and your own financial situation.

How you decide to address these variables will determine your child's spending boundaries. For example, having the ability to buy your kids whatever they want doesn't mean you should. And, if you have two kids, you may discover that one can handle more financial responsibility at a younger age than the other. No one size fits all.

One constant will help bolster your efforts: the Sharing-Saving-Spending philosophy. Adopting this as a guiding principle helps you put spending decisions in the proper perspective.

Shortly after their twin boys started kindergarten, Dave and Barb set guidelines for how their kids spent money. "We felt it was important to talk openly about what kind of stuff they bought. Not to control how they spent every nickel, but more to help them learn how to make good choices," Barb said. According to Barb, many of the early lessons were about setting boundaries. For example, just because a friend could buy an endless supply of candy didn't mean the boys could, too. And just because some parents gave in to every request didn't mean Dave and Barb would do the same.

One advantage for Dave and Barb is that they act as role models for balanced spending. Remember, kids will smoke out incongruity faster than you can say, "Sharing-Saving-Spending."

Track the Flow of Money

The Money In, Money Out exercise in Figure 13.1 is an excellent way for you and your child to compare where you each get your funds and how you each use your money. Complete the exercise separately from your child and then compare your answers. Listing dollar amounts is optional. If you feel it will add an important dimension to the conversation, list away.

A Balanced Life—Spending

Figure 13.1 Money In, Money Out

Each month, I get money from (check all that apply):

❏ Allowance   ❏ Gifts   ❏ Special events
❏ Savings   ❏ Loans   ❏ Other _____
❏ Working   ❏ Investments   _____

Each month, I use my money for (check all that apply):

❏ House/rent payments
❏ Electricity
❏ Natural gas
❏ Garbage
❏ Water/sewage
❏ Telephone
❏ Groceries
❏ Internet
❏ Cell phone
❏ Car payments
❏ Car insurance
❏ Car maintenance
❏ Gas
❏ Payment for boat, cabin, and so on
❏ Charitable donations
❏ Eating meals out

❏ Snacks (chips, soda, candy)
❏ Clothing and shoes
❏ Toiletries (shampoo, cosmetics)
❏ Hair cuts
❏ Prescriptions/ medicines
❏ Laundry/cleaning
❏ Recreation (movies, concerts, CDs)
❏ Newspapers/ periodicals
❏ School supplies and events
❏ Medical insurance
❏ Dental insurance
❏ Life insurance

❏ Disability insurance
❏ Savings
❏ Checking
❏ Investment savings
❏ Other insurance
❏ Credit card balances
❏ Primary education
❏ Secondary education
❏ College education
❏ Adult continuing education
❏ Cable
❏ Other _____
_____
_____
_____

Source: ©2001. Reprinted with permission from Lutheran Brotherhood (now known as Thrivent Financial for Lutherans).

205

This exercise will assist you in three ways:

1. By discussing where money comes from and where it goes, you create a foundation for conversations on needs and wants.
2. You begin to see a connection between your own financial values and habits. Remember, your voice may be the only one your child hears on connecting values with financial decisions.
3. Because you both complete the same sheet, your child will gain a more realistic understanding of your monthly financial obligations. This is also a great counter-rhythm for Teen Commandment Number 10—*Forget Reality*.

Budget with Values in Mind

When you finish the exercise, use your child's new insight as a springboard into discussions on what it means to budget with your values in mind. In Chapter 10, A Balanced Life, I defined a balanced approach to financial matters as aligning your values with how you use your money.

A balanced approach recognizes both the opportunities and responsibilities of sound money management and the interdependence of your own needs and the needs of others. This approach ensures that you and your child consciously address present and future financial issues while building up immunity to unhealthy spontaneous consumption.

I have seen the rewards experienced by families when they set sharing and saving percentages *before* allocating money for spending. This helps you and your child keep on track with the Sharing-Saving-Spending philosophy and keeps you honest with your spending decisions.

Shift the conversation to your child's allowance. Remind your child that she can budget with values in mind by dividing her allowance into three equal parts. Encouraging your child to approach financial issues with this mindset reinforces the Sharing-Saving-Spending philosophy. In the end, setting healthy financial boundaries for young people greatly enhances their prospects for a lifetime of financial success.

Differentiate between a Need and a Want

Earlier in the book I touched on the simple, yet important concept of differentiating between a need and a want. Needs are the basic items required for existence—like food, clothing, and shelter. Essentially, wants are everything else.

Focus on the "Money Out" section in Figure 13.1. Again, complete the exercise separately, then compare your answers. Next to each item listed, put an "N" for need and a "W" for want. You may find that some items are eligible for both. For example, a three-bedroom Cape Cod home might be a need, but a 5000-square-foot, five-bedroom colonial is probably a want. Helping your child understand how the lines can blur is essential in establishing his perspective.

Unless they're told, children don't know the cost of necessities, such as rent or mortgage payments, heat and water, transportation, and other living costs. Parents can show children that needs are paid first and wants are a lower priority.

This really hit home for one woman who called me soon after I finished a television segment for a local news show. As part of my message on teaching children the difference between a need and a want, I encouraged parents to do the "N" and "W" exercise. The woman told me that she and her husband differed in how to begin this conversation with their 7-year-old daughter. She favored a more direct approach, and her husband was more passive. I side with her. Talking about money only gets more difficult if you procrastinate. Straightforward is always the better approach.

Analyze Brand Value

At one of my workshops for middle-school-age young people and their parents, Kathy, a high school math teacher, was having a difficult time helping her sixth-grade son Karl understand the difference between a want and a need. "He usually grasps abstract topics fairly quickly, but in this case he kept thinking brand name clothing was a need," Kathy said.

That's a classic area of confusion. Shoes are a need, but does your child *need* a $150 pair of Doc Martens? Jeans are a need, but does your child *need* an $80 pair of Tommy Hilfigers? For younger kids, do a blind taste test comparing private label or minor brands to major brands in cereal, bread, macaroni and cheese, ice cream, and other foods. For older kids, cut up ads or catalogs for a brand-neutral fashion test. Make sure all labels are covered up, and ask your child to pick the clothes he or she likes best.

Allow Kids to Learn from Their Mistakes

Bailing kids out of little mistakes today can set an unhealthy trend. What begins as a small dollar amount could turn into a many-thousand-dollar credit card bill in the future. The Bank Marketing Association said the average credit card debt of teenagers rose a staggering 300 percent from 1990 to 2000. My hunch is that lots of parents are writing checks to credit card companies.

Monitor Peer Pressure

Peer pressure is a normal part of growing up. But as I described in Chapter 5, the three-headed monster is working overtime to reach young people in virtually every possible location: school, leisure activities, television, radio, and the Internet, to name a few. It is a 24-7 assault to win their affection for a particular brand or lifestyle. Given the stealth marketing tactics that companies use today, monitoring every exchange of consumer-influenced peer pressure will be impossible.

Your best hope for maintaining healthy financial habits and minimizing the "gotta haves" is to stay engaged with your child's needs and wants. If you observe a sudden shift in either the pattern or the type of requests or purchases, ask your child about the change and what might be behind it. In certain situations the change could be legitimate, but in others your child might not be aware that consumer-driven peer pressure has taken hold. Chapter 14, "Raising Your Child's Marketing IQ," is designed to help children recognize when and how they are being manipulated.

Put a Cap on Your Spending Limits

To avoid battles during back-to-school shopping, set a budget and stick to it. Show your child that he can get one pair of trendy jeans and two trendy shirts or two or three pairs of affordable jeans and three or four lower-priced shirts. If having the right brands is so important, your child can pay the premium. Let your child make the choice and live with the decision. Wearing the same pants three days in a week could be embarrassing. The key is to not cave in one month into the school year.

When it comes to distinguishing between wants and needs, beware of the extravagance bug. There will be times when your child insists that he or she needs some expensive item for a special occasion. You may debate the issue, and you always have the right to not pay for it.

Brandon, a senior in high school, was convinced the limo he and a friend were going to rent to surprise their dates for prom was a given. But at $150 an hour, Jack, his father, questioned the decision. "He approached me for the money, and I said, 'Forget it.' I know times are different, but that bill alone was going to be a few hundred dollars," Jack said.

Brandon countered by saying "all his friends" were renting limos. He ultimately dropped the request and used the family car. Good for Jack, who refused to contribute to extravagence, and good for Brandon, who accepted a reasonable alternative rather than strain his finances on a luxury.

Invite Other Relatives to Help

As I detailed in Chapter 6, Where's the Rest of the Village?, relatives can be unknowing collaborators with the three-headed monster. Parents repeatedly tell me how tough it is combating the external consumer influences on their child. When it spills over to grandparents, aunts, uncles, and other family members, the topic can be emotionally charged.

I suggest leveraging your relatives as allies in your effort to achieve financial balance. Andrea encouraged her dad to be a steady reinforcer of her family's financial values. "Dad was an excellent financial role model for me growing up, and I thought he could be an excellent advocate for our kids," said Andrea. A 10-10-80 believer (percentages for sharing, saving, and spending), he never preaches to the kids. Rather, he lets his actions create opportunities for conversations. Instead of feeding the consumer machine at birthdays, he spends time with the kids doing something educational.

Understand Your Child's Unique Money Temperament

Every child has one. How many times have you heard someone say, "He's a real spender" or "She's definitely a saver"? The earlier you can identify your child's temperament, the more prepared you will be to teach him about money, especially spending.

When I wrote the workshop, "Parents, Kids & Money,"

in 1990, I wanted an ice breaker to pull the kids into the experience and created an idea still used today: I hand each child a play $100 bill and ask them to draw a picture of how they would use their new money. (Notice I said *use*, not spend. It's an important distinction.) Over the next five minutes each child draws all kinds of interesting pictures.

What follows is a chance for each child to share how he or she would use the money. In explaining their decisions, they reveal their money temperament. I have heard everything from, "I'm putting it all in the bank" to "I'm buying a new convertible" to "I'm giving it to a homeless shelter." One young man shocked his parents and declared that he was going to buy a king snake.

The exercise always gives parents keen insight into how their child thinks about money. If you have a spender, you'll need an observant eye on emerging consumer habits. If you have a saver, you may need to help your child understand it's okay to spend money. If your child shares too generously, you may have to remind her to meet her own needs as well.

You may recall how I highlighted Tracy and Bruce and their son, Jason. He was the spender of their two kids, which the parents detected by age 7. Younger brother Peter is a voracious saver. "Recently, we discovered he had over $100 in his saving jar and immediately made a trip to the bank. Every so often we have to remind him that it's okay to spend some of his money," said Tracy.

Balance is best. Too much of one thing (sharing, saving, or spending) can be a sign that you need to intervene. Don't be surprised if your child has a dominant characteristic. As long as you understand that tendency, you can have great success.

Discuss Your Spending Goals

Especially when you plan a major spending goal, like a vacation, a new car, or a new computer, talk with your children about how you make a financial decision. Let them in on how much things cost, and share with them how you plan to pay for it. I'm convinced that if more parents did this, there would be much less credit card debt.

When I was growing up, I have vivid memories of my parents telling us they were saving for our family vacation. They wanted to establish it as a family goal so we could celebrate the accomplishment, but they also saw it as a way to build excitement for the trip. As another benefit of telling us their plans early, we set aside trip money from our allowance. Even though it was for spending, it reinforced short-term savings goals.

Encourage Good Decisions

Because so much energy encourages your child to make questionable spending decisions, go out of your way to acknowledge them when they exercise restraint. The power of reinforcement is a wonderful thing. One mother shared with me that, after her son started his first part-time job, he became even more diligent about stretching his money by comparison shopping and looking for value. She said it was because he felt responsibility for managing his own money. Obviously, she did something right along the way as well.

Encourage Patience

Virtually everything goes on sale if you're willing to wait. Whether it's clothing or some other item with a premium brand, paying full price can be an unnecessary waste of money.

Luke, a 14-year-old, used his money to buy the new Nintendo GameCube, a video game console. He bought it in October, a week after it came out, for $200. Approximately six months after the release, Nintendo cut the price by $50.

Ouch! I asked him how he felt after he learned of the sale. "Not good. I should have waited because the games cost $50," Luke said.

As hard as it might seem, teaching your child to be patient can be a valuable lesson for a couple of reasons. First, you can smoke out his true interest in a "gotta-have" item. Second, he learns deferred gratification.

A single mom with three kids instituted a 24-hour waiting period before anybody in the family makes a big spending decision. Of course, big is relative to the child's age. Regardless, it has helped everyone, Mom included, curb the craving for immediate gratification.

Maintaining Balance

A word of caution: Because so much of your child's day focuses on ways to spend money, many parents tend to weight their conversations on money toward spending. Be aware that talking mostly about spending may take away from important conversations on sharing and saving.

Other Resources

National Council on Economic Education (www.italladdsup.org)
    "It All Adds Up" is a Web-based, interactive program designed to help teens get a head start on their financial future. The site includes online games and simulations to learn about credit management, buying a car, paying for college, budgeting, saving, and investing.

JumpStart Coalition (www.jumpstartcoalition.org)
    JumpStart is dedicated to teaching young adults the fundamentals of financial literacy. The organization has an interactive exercise called the Reality Check, which helps young people understand just how much money it

takes to live on their own. JumpStart also maintains (with the help of the National Institute for Consumer Education) a searchable database of personal finance educational materials.

Consumer Reports Online for Kids (www.zillions.org)

Consumer Reports for Kids is the junior version of the popular web site for adults. There are money Q&A's, product reviews by kids, interactive exercises, and fun polls.

Money Talks

- Do you really need this item or is it just a want?
- If it's something you need, what makes you think you need it?
- If it's something you want, why do you want it?
- Will you need or want this thing a month from now? Six months from now?
- Is it a good use of your money?

Chapter FOURTEEN

Raising Your Child's Marketing IQ

In October 2000, for the first time in more than 40 years, the World Series was contested by New York City rivals, the Mets and Yankees. Just my luck, on the evening of game four, I was scheduled to do a workshop for several hundred middle-school-age kids and their parents on Long Island. Although I was hopeful, I wasn't expecting a great turnout.

As it turns out, it was standing room only. Not for the game, but for the interactive workshop, "Your Money, Your Message." The goal of the program was to inform young people that they were a primary target for advertising and other marketing efforts. More specifically, we wanted them to know that there are carefully planned campaigns aimed at influencing their financial habits and values. The kids showed such terrific interest that you would have never guessed they cared about missing the game.

A panel of kids dissected commercials. Group exercises helped sort through the difference between needs and wants. The kids also discovered how the three-headed monster could be a big-time roadblock in achieving financial balance. The more kids and parents learned together, the more intrigued and angry they were about being manipulated by highly choreographed advertising messages.

Jerry, a concerned parent of two teenage boys, approached me after the workshop and described how challenging it was to find support for teaching kids financial balance. "More organizations need to recognize this as a vital skill for young people and their future. I didn't learn this stuff at their age, but I wasn't bombarded with commercials at every turn, either," said Jerry. The boys' local school had dabbled in the subject, but he was pressing them to do more.

Turning the Tables

The first part of this book detailed the extremes to which some companies go to shape a young person's financial values. Advertising and other tools of the three-headed monster press young people's emotional buttons and cleverly distort and confuse the difference between a need and a want.

Sometimes a company's clever tactics can backfire. The creators of the anti-tobacco commercials have helped young people use similar persuasive marketing tactics and turn it right back on tobacco companies. The result is that some states have seen significant declines in teen smoking. Is it possible we could someday see anti-exploitation ads that target the three-headed monster?

Ultimately, the more your kids know, the better equipped they will be at recognizing when and how they are being manipulated. By pointing out youth-focused marketing tactics, you can awaken an important curiosity in your child, one that constantly questions the why and the how behind the message.

Consider this a primer on analyzing marketing messages. If you incorporate the following suggestions into your regular routine of money talks, your child will gain the necessary ability to see through marketing tactics.

They're Everywhere

To stimulate conversation, create a Marketing Jar—or, if you prefer, a Three-Headed Monster Jar. It works like this: I encourage both parents and young people to document all the different kinds of marketing that targets young people—anything that highlights a brand name or encourages young people to spend money. Write it on a slip of paper, and stuff it in the jar. The goal: See how long it takes to fill the jar. This family project sensitizes everyone to the variety and volume of marketing energy directed at young people. Don't forget to read all the slips as a family.

Some obvious examples are TV commercials, peer pressure, magazine ads, and product placement, especially in TV shows and video games. Actually, the sky's the limit—blimps and planes with banners count, too! What about the not-so-obvious? Bathroom stall advertising has grown exponentially. Every sporting event is a nonstop commercial. So too are concerts, movies and, yes, even schools. Some child marketing experts say a lifetime customer may be worth $100,000 to a retailer, making effective "cradle to grave" strategies extremely valuable.[1]

You may also want to test the success of your discussions. Before you introduce the jar, decide which of the Teen Commandments, described in Chapter 4, apply to your child. After the jar fills, do another assessment to see if the frequent discussions have had an effect on your child's attitudes.

Play the Name Game

As another way to help your child recognize the presence of marketing, try this variation on the games you may have played during a car trip. When driving your children through a commercial area, ask them to find ways that company or product names are displayed. They're likely to see billboards, neon signs, banners, storefronts, signs on taxis, ads on buses and bus benches, service vans, delivery trucks, bumper stickers, uniforms, and more. You can do the same thing at a sporting event, where signs are everywhere and companies sponsor activities and features in the event program, such as the roster, scorecard, and player profiles. Remember, the home team is a product, too.

You could even challenge the kids to count the marketing intrusions during a 30-minute program. Watch for product placements, a network logo, and other promotional messages superimposed on the screen, and additional advertising that nudges aside the ending credits. That ought to help the kids realize how marketing surrounds them. Note that seeing a name doesn't guarantee it's a good company or product.

Name That Ploy

Advertisers commonly use the following techniques, according to "Media and the Marketplace," a LifeSmarts Internet Lesson on the Minnesota Attorney General's web site. Explain these to your child and ask your child to recall ads they have seen or heard that employ each technique. The next time you watch TV with your child, try to identify what the ads really say.

1. **"Cool" factor.** If you buy this, you too will have fun, be popular, look hot, run fast, or be cool. For example, if you own a skateboard or a snowboard, Vans would have you think that owning the company's shoes, clothing, and other accessories is the key to cool. You might be a novice on the board, but you will make a statement that says "I belong."

2. **Bandwagon.** Everyone who's anyone uses this. If you don't buy it, you may as well stamp "not cool" on your forehead. Sprite's campaign, "Obey your thirst," has been mega-successful. Coca-Cola invested millions of dollars in events and promotions to establish Sprite as the "in" beverage of teens and tweens. Imagine that—you too can be part of the cool crowd by drinking flavored sugar water.

3. **Celebrity testimonial.** I'm a superstar and I love this, so you will too! And if you want to be as athletic, beautiful, or famous as me, you should buy it. Michael Jordan has made multimillions for himself and Nike as he convinced tons of kids to buy his overpriced shoes and apparel.

4. **Emotion.** Because I bought this, I feel a certain way. You should buy this so that you too can feel happy, confident, secure, or loved. Procter & Gamble, the consumer products giant, spends upwards of $30 million/year advertising in teen magazines. As detailed in Chapter 5, the company goes to great lengths to convince insecure girls that Cover Girl beauty products will make the difference.

5. **Expert testimonial.** I know my stuff, and I'm telling you, this is just what you need. In one study, one-third of children believed cartoon characters were recommending cereal because they were nutrition experts. The "experts"— Fred Flintstone and Barney Rubble—were pitching vitamins. Young children do not have the ability to understand what is real and what is fiction.

6. **Repetition.** Didn't notice this at first? Maybe after the millionth time you see it, you'll be singing the jingle or reciting the commercial in your sleep. "Did somebody say McDonalds?" Can you hear the tune in your head yet? McDonald's might be the all-time master of how to push kids' buttons. The company knows who pulls Mom and Dad in and pursues them with a vengeance.

7. **Slogan.** A catchy phrase sticks in your head. You can even recite the phrase without seeing the ad. When you hear, "Wassuuuup?" you immediately remember Budweiser and its humor-filled ads for beer. In its heyday, it was the most popular ad of kids *under* age 17. An 8-year-old girl from Moline, Illinois, said, "I know I'm not old enough to drink beer, but if I could, it would definitely be a Budweiser." Now there's a comforting thought.

Reality Check

Now that your children have identified specific ads, efforts, or situations that target them, take it to the next level by asking specific questions:

- What techniques did the ad use to make you identify with the situation or characters?
- How did the ad make you feel?
- What words or phrases made the product sound appealing?
- What techniques were used to make the product look appealing?
- What did the setting or props convey?
- If the ad used humor, for what reason?
- Do you think the product is as good as it looks in the ad?

Turn Off the Tube

Why is the most obvious answer always the easiest to forget? Because once again it's a habit and, good or bad, it's hard to break. Each year the average child spends 900 hours in school and 1500 hours in front of a television.[2]

In Chapter 10, I mentioned how Ted and Diane used the Sharing-Saving-Spending philosophy to introduce their kids to allowances. For several years, the approach has been working well, aided by the fact that Ted and Diane limit the amount of television their three boys watch. "Television is not an automatic in our house. Not only are some of the shows questionable, we don't want them exposed to the nonstop advertising," said Ted. Although they wonder if they are sheltering the boys too much, they have noticed a reduction in their anxiety level since they cut back on Saturday morning cartoons. I think it's an excellent decision, since most Saturday morning shows have adopted the MTV formula, where everything is one big advertisement.

According to a Yankelovich Monitor survey, eight in ten parents make it their business to know exactly what TV programs their children watch. That's an encouraging sign, but what about commercials? Are parents monitoring what commercials their kids watch? Studies show that kids are much more likely than adults to sit through commercials. Advertising companies know it. So the next time you get up for a beverage during a commercial break, consider bringing your child along.

A License to Sell

Chapter 3 detailed the efforts of companies to push licensed products. Fast-food restaurants have used this ploy for years. Consider the reason your child asks to go to McDonald's or Burger King. Is it the burger? Or the licensed toy that is connected to a movie that is connected to a Saturday morning TV show that is connected to some other toy?

Dr. Dave Walsh, founder and president of the National Institute on Media and the Family, created a simple exercise to identify the prevalence of licensed products in the home of a child age 5 to 12. Easy to identify, licensed products link products with television shows, movies, video games, the Internet, or other forms of mass media. I suggest you try Dr. Walsh's exercise to see how many licensed products are regular parts of your child's world. Dr. Walsh suggests you do the following:

1. Survey the toys and other products your child owns. Check those that are linked to television shows, movies, or video games. Don't be surprised if you have multiple checks for each line.

_____ Action figures   _____ Dress-up sets
_____ Dolls   _____ Guns/Weapons
_____ Animal figures   _____ Wrestling figures
_____ Monster and space   _____ Action sets or props for
      figures   action figures

2. Check other products you buy that are linked to media characters:

_____ Toothpaste   _____ Bed linens
_____ Food   _____ Snacks
_____ School supplies   _____ Clothes
_____ Shoes   _____ Hats

Source: Reprinted with the permission of Simon & Schuster Adult Publishing Group from [DR. DAVE'S CYBERHOOD] by David Walsh, PhD. Copyright ©2000 by National Institute on Media and the Family.

Rarely will you ever see a children's movie, TV show, or video game that isn't heavily cross-marketed. Once again, by knowing what you're up against, you can devise an effective strategy to counter the effects of the hypnotic pull. This might mean monitoring the depth of licensed products you are willing to accept. On this slippery slope, where your child always wants one more thing with a Yu-Gi-Oh!

image, the best solution might be to avoid licensed products altogether.

Other Resources

PBS Kids—"Don't Buy It" (www.pbskids.org/dontbuyit)

This is a fun, new PBS site that gives the scoop on tricks that advertisers play on you. It features interactive lessons that your kids and you will find fascinating. Discover the secrets of advertising. Learn how to question a commercial. Get a behind-the-scenes look at TV, music, and magazines.

PBS Frontline—"Merchants of Cool" (www.pbs.org/frontline; search word: cool)

Frontline journeys into the world of the marketers—the merchants of cool—who popularize teenage culture. The web site and the television special expose the creepy side of the three-headed monster. They talk to kids, media executives, market researchers, and cultural critics about living in a world dominated by marketing messages.

National Institute on Media and the Family (www.mediaandthe family.org)

This organization is for parents and educators interested in the influence of media on children. Resources include media awareness programs and content ratings for movies, television shows, and video games. You'll also find helpful hints to evaluate use of media.

Center for a New American Dream (www.newdream.org)

The Center works to conserve natural resources, counter the commercialization of our culture, and promote positive changes in the way goods are produced and consumed. An excellent web site, it offers tips and links plus an opportunity to gain insight from other parents.

223

PBS Affluenza (www.pbs.org/affluenza)
    Affluenza is a one-hour television special that explores the high social and environmental costs of materialism and overconsumption. At the web site you can learn more about the show, get an Affluenza diagnosis and check out resources for treatment. There are also excellent guides for parents and teachers.

The Center for Media Literacy (www.medialit.org)
    The organization strives to help people access, understand, analyze, and evaluate the powerful images, words, and sounds that make up our contemporary mass media culture. They have a great online catalog that features a "best of" selection of educational materials.

Money Talks

- Do you see value in discussing ads with your child?
- Do you think companies are increasing their efforts in targeting young people?
- Are companies effective at influencing the consumer decisions of your child?
- Will improving your knowledge of various marketing tactics help in your quest for teaching financial balance?
- Have you tried limiting the amount of television your child watches and, if so, did it help reduce the nag factor?

Chapter FIFTEEN

Learning to Fly before Leaving the Nest

L ike most 17-year-old high school seniors, Hans cele-
brated his graduation with a party for family and
friends, works a part-time job, and can't wait to head to
college in the fall. But, after spending some time with him,
you discover he has a few unique qualities for someone his
age, especially when it comes to money.

Hans is a thinker. He thinks about what he reads, hears,
and observes. Over the years, he has observed and listened
to his parents and other role models on the values of sharing, saving, and spending. He also is wise to the enormous
amounts of consumer energy directed his way. "I get really
annoyed at all the commercials pushed at people my age to
buy stuff. So often it's for a bunch of stuff we don't need,"
Hans said.

For Hans, the balanced philosophy has taken hold. In
Chapter 11, I mentioned that his parents, Leslee and Jim,
were surprised and touched when they discovered he do-
nated 10 percent of his earnings to their church. "I decided

to share 10 percent because I wanted to do my part," Hans said. "It makes me feel good, and I never miss the money."

Hans also has learned the art of deferred gratification and saving for a goal—like his first car. He can describe in detail his first toy bank. "It was red, and when you dropped coins in it, they would land in various slots, depending on their size. I would put my allowance money in there until I needed it for something," said Hans. Now he has both checking and savings accounts and is considering starting a Roth IRA when he turns 18.

"I know I'm young, but I don't worry about money because I feel I have a good system," Hans said. "It doesn't mean I don't make mistakes, but I try to learn from them and do better next time." He admits to wanting a credit card—not to buy stuff he can't afford but to build his credit rating, a lesson he learned in his high school economics course. His financial vocabulary is impressive and rivals many adults'.

Not an Accident

Hans didn't develop values-based financial habits overnight. They were nurtured through years of teachable moments woven into a multitude of deliberate conversations. Although they deflect any credit, his parents played starring roles with a strong supporting cast of interested mentors. They lead by example and back it up with persistent words of encouragement.

Like most of us, they occasionally slip up and make mistakes with how they use their money. But at the end of the day, they maintain a consistent rhythm to their dialogue on issues relating to money. "I have total confidence in Hans' ability to handle money," Jim said. What parent wouldn't want to make that declaration as your child takes the next step toward independence?

Leverage Your Knowledge

Knowing what you are up against and understanding how external forces shape a young person's financial habits and values may be the most important information you take from this book. When you combine that knowledge with some of the suggestions from Part II, I hope they will become part of your family's normal rhythm in talking and teaching about money.

By committing to a plan and taking the all-important first step, the second and third will be that much easier. While I know a lot of issues compete for your time, many teachable moments pass in front of you every day.

You can build your child's financial confidence and discipline by leveraging your newfound knowledge, skills, and insight. Help make them healthy skeptics. If your kids merely stop and ask questions before acting, they won't be puppets controlled by advertising and peer pressure. They will be savvy consumers who make decisions based on their values.

There might be times when you think your efforts are not working. In those moments of doubt or disappointment, remember the saying, "If at first you don't succeed, try, try again." Persistence will always be your greatest ally.

Balanced Financial Values + Healthy Financial Habits = Sustainable Boundaries = Financial Success

You may not have the muscle and the might of those trying to influence your children's habits, but you do have time, actions, and a philosophy to shore up their skills. Perhaps most importantly, remember you have a captive audience. Because everything we do with money has some kind of value attached to it, you face endless opportunities to demonstrate the link of your financial decisions to your financial values. And by committing to the process, you are establishing important routines and boundaries to your child's present and future financial decisions. All of these elements are critical for lasting financial success.

Share—Save—Spend

While individually these are three simple words, put them together and the potential for financial success is powerful. By incorporating these words and their order into your daily financial routine, the lasting value for your child could be dramatic. To energize you for the journey, let me offer a few final words of encouragement:

- Use teachable moments to incorporate new ideas.
- Let your financial philosophy guide big and small decisions.
- Invest the time to be a good role model and mentor.
- Use allowance to teach responsibility and accountability.
- Look and listen for other creative, successful ideas. They're all around you.
- Treat the subject seriously, but have fun along the way.

Whether young or old, of modest means or wealthy, time and again I have seen people successfully adopt this simple yet proven philosophy. In virtually every situation, the formula for financial success has been the same: a committed depth of generosity; financial goals that are met repeatedly; and contentment with the stuff they really need. The Sharing-Saving-Spending philosophy will serve you well as you talk with your child about money. Even though it may be a while before your child realizes what you have done, seeing them transition into adulthood with balanced financial values will give you reason to celebrate.

A New Spirit of Generosity

By some twist of fate, I was there—in lower Manhattan, attending a marketing conference—on September 11, 2001. I will never forget what I saw or what I experienced, but even more powerful than those hellish memories was the amazing generosity of New Yorkers and people all across the country.

In the first 24 hours, I witnessed hundreds of intentional acts of kindness. Whether it was giving money, time, or blood, people immediately thought beyond themselves and shared. During our lifetimes, we may never again feel such a universal need to help people we don't even know. But let's never forget that feeling.

In the best possible outcome from that horrific event, we would continue to act with a September 12 mindset and remember the needs of others. Millions of people around the world still live in need. By adjusting our priorities, we can both help more people through sharing and help ourselves by clarifying the role money plays in our lives.

The people around us will notice this mindset—the spirit of generosity and the thought-filled approach to sharing, saving, and spending. I hope you embrace the opportunity and give your child a lifetime of financial balance. Pass it on!

Notes

Chapter ONE   Just Buy It!

1. "Undergraduate Students and Credit Cards," a report published by Nellie Mae, April 2002, at www.nelliemae.com.
2. "Marketing to Kids Taking Its Toll on Parents," a survey commissioned for the Center for a New American Dream, July 1999, at www.newdream.org.
3. Ibid.
4. Kelly, Katy, "Making Allowances for Your Kids' Dollar Values," *U.S. News & World Report*, February 12, 2000.
5. Ibid.
6. Miller, Kay, "Charging into Debt Triggers Student Anxiety," *Minneapolis Star Tribune*, September 21, 1999.
7. Dugas, Christine, "Debt Smothers Young Americans," *USA Today*, February 13, 2001.
8. U.S. Department of Commerce, Bureau of Economic Analysis, "Personal Saving as a Percentage of After Tax Investing," at www.bea.doc.gov.
9. Dugas, "Debt Smothers Young Americans."
10. Haddad, Charles, "Congratulations, Grads—You're Bankrupt," *BusinessWeek*, May 21, 2001.

11. Dugas, "Debt Smothers Young Americans."

12. "Facts and Figures about Our TV Habit," TV Turnoff Network at www.tvfa.org.

Chapter TWO   The Gotta-Have-It-Now Generation

1. "Useful Back to School Planning Tips from the ICFE," Institute of Consumer Financial Education at www.financial -education-icfe.org.

2. Kantrowitz, Barbara, and Pat Wingert, "The Truth about Tweens," *Newsweek*, October 18, 1999.

3. May, Gerald G., *Addiction and Grace* (New York: Harper & Row, 1988), p. 24.

4. Ibid., p. 26.

5. Dungan, Rev. Alvin, "Addiction, Recovery and Pastoral Ministry," January 2001.

6. May, *Addiction and Grace,* p. 28.

7. "College Students and Money," a survey by Harris Interactive for Lutheran Brotherhood, July 2001.

8. May, *Addiction and Grace,* p. 28.

9. Dungan, Rev. Alvin, "Addiction, Recovery and Pastoral Ministry."

10. Ibid.

11. Ibid.

12. "Teen Struggle with Peer Pressure," California State University study at www.csus.edu.

13. "From Bad to Worse: Financial Literacy Drops Further among 12th Graders," JumpStart Coalition for Personal Financial Literacy, April 23, 2002, at www.jumpstart.org.

Chapter THREE   A Branded New World

1. Kaiser Family Foundation, "Kids and Media at the New Millennium," November 1999.

2. McNeal, James, *The Kids Market: Myths and Realities* (Ithaca, NY: Paramount Market Publishing, 1999), p. 96.

3. Wellner Stein, Alison, "The Power of the Purse," *American Demographics*, July/August 2002.
4. McNeal, *The Kids Market,* p. 88.
5. Ibid., p. 92.
6. Relly, Jeannine, "Generation Y: Corporations, Local Retailers Focus on Vast Pool of Teen, Pre-Teen Buyers," *Arizona Daily Star*, April 15, 2001.
7. Cohen, Marsha, and the Editors of *Youth Markets Alert, Marketing to Teens and Tweens* (New York: EPM Communications, 2001), p. 2.
8. Relly, "Generation Y."
9. McNeal, James U., "Tapping the Three Kids' Markets," *American Demographics*, April 1998.
10. Relly, "Generation Y."
11. Euromonitor, "Marketing to Children: A World Survey," at www.euromonitor.com.
12. Broad, William J., "Engineer at Play: Lonnie Johnson; Rocket Science, Served Up Soggy," *New York Times*, July 31, 2001.
13. Olenick, Doug, "Video Games, Early Learning Aids Power Toy Industry," *Twice*, 17 (5): 38 (February 25, 2002).
14. Cohen et al., *Marketing to Teens and Tweens*, p. 49.
15. Thomas, Donald A., Jr., "I.C. When, The Chronological History of Video Games and Computers," at www.icwhen.com.
16. Alexander, Steve, "Playing for Keeps," *Star Tribune*, May 20, 2002.
17. Cohen et al., *Marketing to Teens and Tweens*, p. 24.
18. Ibid., p. 49.
19. Pappas, Ben, "Star Bucks," *Forbes*, May 17, 1999.
20. "Sesame Workshop and International Growth," American Graduate School of International Management, at www.t-bird.edu.
21. Angrisani, Carol, "What a Doll," *Brandmarketing* VI (6): 1+ (June 1999).
22. Hume, Scott, "Top 400 Chains," *Restaurants and Institutions*, July 15, 2001.
23. Cohen et al., *Marketing to Teens and Tweens*, p. 44.
24. Askari, Emilia, "Marketing to Younger Tastes: Kids Eat Up Fast-Food Ad Blitz," *Detroit Free Press*, April 8, 2002.

25. Ibid.
26. McNeal, *The Kids Market*, p. 201.
27. Askari, "Marketing to Younger Tastes."
28. Ibid.
29. Ibid.
30. Cohen et al., *Marketing to Teens and Tweens*, p. 43.
31. Cullen, Karen, Danielle M. Ash, Carla Warneke, and Carl de Moor, "Intake of Soft Drinks, Fruit-Flavored Beverages, and Fruits and Vegetables by Children in Grades 4 through 6," *American Journal of Public Health* 2002, 92: 1475–1477.
32. Crespo, Carlos J., et al., "Television Watching, Energy Intake, and Obesity in U.S. Children," *Archives of Pediatric and Adolescent Medicine*, March 15, 2001, pp. 155, 360–365.
33. Centers for Disease Control, "Physical Activity and Youth" (2000). Available online at www.cdc.gov/kidsmedia/background.htm.
34. Crespo et al., "Television Watching, Energy Intake, and Obesity in U.S. Children."
35. Tenerelli, Mary Jane, "Dressing Three Generations with Success," *Body Fashions Intimate Apparel*, 30 (11): 18+ (November 2000).
36. Cohen et al., *Marketing to Teens and Tweens*, p. 29.
37. Ibid., p. 36.
38. www.vans.com.
39. Cohen et al., *Marketing to Teens and Tweens*, p. 37.
40. Ibid.
41. Ang, Peggy, "Sony Walkman: A Case Study in Revitalizing Brands for Today's Youth Market," Talking to Teens Conference, New York, January 25, 2002.
42. Sapp, Taeyma, and Michael Arndt, "The New Burger Wars: Backstreet Boys vs. Britney," BusinessWeek Online, September 14, 2000.
43. Cohen et al., *Marketing to Teens and Tweens*, p. 92.
44. "Cell Phone Now Status Symbol for Teens," at www.channelcinncinati.com, October 19, 2001.
45. Cohen et al., *Marketing to Teens and Tweens*, p. 94.
46. Ibid., p. 81.

47. Ibid., p. 88.

48. www.vans.com.

49. Cohen et al., *Marketing to Teens and Tweens*, p. 36.

50. Ibid.

51. Ibid., p. 34.

52. Ibid., p. 35.

53. www.mallofamerica.com.

54. Ibid.

55. Cohen et al., *Marketing to Teens and Tweens*, p. 35.

56. "Who's Hot in Retail," *Shopping Centers Today*, October 1, 2000.

57. Ibid.

58. Hazel, Debra, "Pacific Sunwear Rides Trends from Surf to Street," *Shopping Centers Today*, December 1, 1998.

59. Pena, Elisabeth, "New Retail Concepts Target Teen and Preteen Girls," ESP, the News Report for Entertainment, Specialty, Projects at www.specialtyretail.net.

60. "In Brief: Seventeen Spa and Salon," *Women's Wear Daily*, 183 (35): 2 (February 21, 2002).

61. Cohen et al., *Marketing to Teens and Tweens*, p. 89.

62. Woods, Bob, "Linking Up with Wired Youth," *Chief Executive*, March 2002.

63. www.visabuxx.com.

64. Nugent, Meg, "Teen Plastic: Debit Cards Offered to Kids," Newhouse News Service, November 2, 2000.

65. Ibid.

Chapter FOUR   The Teen Commandments

1. White, Erin, "Racy Lingerie Is Hot New Fashion, but Is It Too Sexy for Teenage Girls?" *Wall Street Journal*, August 3, 2001.

2. "Connecting with Kids," *Restaurant Hospitality*, 86 (4): 32 (April 2002).

3. "Tanning Beds Raise Cancer Risk," *Journal of the National Cancer Institute* 2002, 94: 224.

4. "Dangers of Anabolic Steroids," at www.kidshealth.org.

5. "Number of Cosmetic Procedures Performed Grows 48% from 2000 to 2001," *Research Alert*, 20 (5): 1+ (March 1, 2002).

Chapter FIVE   The Three-Headed Monster

1. Klein, N., *No Logo: Taking Aim at the Brand Bullies* (New York: Picador, 1999), pp. 66–68.
2. Knox, S., "Social Network Marketing—The Power of the Connector," Talking to Teens Conference, New York, January 25, 2002.
3. Ibid.
4. Ibid.
5. Ibid.
6. Ibid.
7. Ibid.
8. News release: "Thanks to Ads, Kids Won't Take No, No, No, No . . . for an Answer," Center for a New American Dream, May 2002, at www.newdream.org.
9. www.newdream.org.
10. Banfe, E., "So What Do We Do Now? . . . Introducing Your Company to the Teen Market," Talking to Teens Conference, New York, January 25, 2002.
11. Cohen, Marsha, and the Editors of *Youth Markets Alert, Marketing to Teens and Tweens* (New York: EPM Communications, 2001), p. 8.
12. Neuborne, Ellen, "For Kids on the Web, It's an Ad, Ad, Ad, Ad World," *BusinessWeek*, August 13, 2001.
13. Ibid.
14. Cohen et al., *Marketing to Teens and Tweens*, p. 60.
15. "Nike Launches $200 Air Jordan Shoe," February 1, 2002, at www.CBSNews.com.
16. Cohen et al., *Marketing to Teens and Tweens*, p. 73.
17. News release: "Procter & Gamble and Viacom Plus Announce Major Marketing Partnership," May 31, 2001, at www.viacom.com.
18. Dobrow, Larry, "How Old Is Enough?" *Advertising Age*, 73: S4 (February 4, 2002).
19. Capell, Kerry, "MTV's World," *BusinessWeek*, February 18, 2002.
20. "The Merchants of Cool: A Report on the Creators and Marketers of Popular Culture for Teenagers," PBS *Frontline* at www.pbs.org.

21. Ibid.
22. Ibid.
23. Ibid.
24. Jackson, Derrick Z., "Hollywood and Madison Avenue Need to Be Reined In," *The Boston Globe*, September 13, 2000.
25. Ibid.
26. Ibid.
27. "The Merchants of Cool."
28. Ibid.
29. Azzarone, Stephanie, quoted at www.childsplaypr.com.
30. Ibid.
31. News release: www.newdream.org.
32. Clay, Rebecca, "Advertising to Children: Is It Ethical?" *Monitor on Psychology*, 31: 8 (September 2000).
33. Ibid.
34. Acuff, D., *What Kids Buy and Why: The Psychology of Marketing to Kids*, (New York: Free Press, 1997), p. 5.
35. Clay, "Advertising to Children."
36. Ibid.
37. Ibid.
38. Ibid.
39. Milligan, Katie, quoted at www.newdream.org.
40. Ibid.
41. Jackson, "Hollywood and Madison Avenue Need to Be Reined In."
42. Cohen et al., *Marketing to Teens and Tweens*, p. 25.
43. Voight, Joan, "Adweek 2000: The Consumer Rebellion," *Adweek*, January 10, 2000.
44. Ibid.

Chapter SIX   Where's the Rest of the Village?

1. Clinton, Hillary, *It Takes a Village, and Other Lessons Children Teach Us* (New York: Simon & Schuster, 1996), p. 12.
2. Ibid., p. 11.
3. "From Bad to Worse: Financial Literacy Drops Further among 12th Graders," JumpStart Coalition for Personal Financial Literacy, April 23, 2002, at www.jumpstart.org.

4. "What We Need to Know about $," *Parade*, April 18, 1999.
5. Ibid.
6. Baker, Russ, "Stealth TV," *American Prospect*, 12: 3 (February 12, 2001).
7. Ibid.
8. Ruskin, Gary, "Let's Keep Advertising and Market Research out of the Classroom," as quoted at www.nsba.com.
9. Feen, Diane, "$150B Youth Market Provides Lure for PR," *O'Dwyer's PR Services Report*, 14: 1 (January 2000).
10. Lay, Donald, "Reaching the All Important Teen Audience through In-School Marketing," Talking to Teens Conference, New York, January 23, 2002.
11. Ibid.
12. Ibid.
13. Ibid.
14. Ibid.
15. Ibid.
16. Ibid.
17. Kaufman, Marc, "Fighting the Cola Wars in Schools," *Washington Post*, March 23, 1999.
18. Ibid.
19. Manning, R., *Credit Card Nation: The Consequences of America's Addiction to Credit* (New York: Basic Books, 2000), p. 162.
20. Ibid.
21. Ibid., p. 9.
22. Ibid., p. 304.
23. Ibid., p. 167.
24. Nader, Ralph, "Congress Protects Those Who Prey on Children," Knight Ridder/Tribune News Service, September 21, 1999.
25. Starek, Commissioner Roscoe B., III, "The ABCs at the FTC: Marketing and Advertising to Children," Minnesota Institute of Legal Education, Minneapolis, Minnesota, July 25, 1997.
26. Ibid.
27. MacKinnon, James, "Psychologists Act against Ad Doctors," *Adbusters*, Winter 2000.
28. Ruskin, Gary, quoted at www.commercialalert.org.

29. www.opensecrets.org.
30. Wuthnow, Robert, *Rethinking Materialism: Perspectives on the Spiritual Dimension of Economic Behavior* (Grand Rapids: Eerdmans, 1995), p. 3.
31. Roehlkepartain, Eugene C., Elanah Dalyah Naftali, and Laura Musegades, *Growing Up Generous: Engaging Youth in Giving and Serving* (Bethesda: Alban Institute, 2000), p. 38.
32. Ibid., p. 41.
33. Wuthnow, Robert, *God and Mammon in America* (New York: Free Press, 1994), p. 119.
34. Roehlkepartain et al., *Growing Up Generous,* p. 44.
35. Wuthnow, *God and Mammon in America,* p. 151.
36. Roehlkepartain et al., *Growing Up Generous,* p. 45.
37. Ibid.
38. Ibid., p. 48.
39. Ibid., p. 50.
40. Ibid., p. 52.
41. Ibid.
42. Marcotty, Josephine, "Legislature Ponders Survival of Edgy Anti-tobacco Campaign," *Minneapolis Star Tribune,* March 26, 2002.
43. Paul, Pamela, "Make Room for Granddaddy," *American Demographics,* 24: 4 (April 2002).

Chapter SEVEN   Your Own Worst Enemy

1. Queripel, Mark, and Theresa Queripel, "Millennium Trends," *Denver Post,* January 21, 2001.
2. Lim, Paul J., and Matthew Benjamin, "Digging Your Way Out of Debt," *U.S. News & World Report,* March 19, 2001.
3. De Graaf, John, David Wann, and Thomas H. Naylor, *Affluenza: The All-Consuming Epidemic* (San Francisco: Berrett-Koehler, 2001), p. 2.
4. Goldman, Debra, "Paradox of Pleasure," *American Demographics,* May 1999.
5. Palmer, Jay, "Taking Off the White Gloves," *Barron's,* April 1, 2002.

6. Goldman, Debra, "Paradox of Pleasure."

7. Ibid.

8. Schor, Juliet B., *The Overspent American: Why We Want What We Don't Need* (New York: HarperPerennial, 1998), p. 76.

9. De Graaf et al., *Affluenza*, p. 32.

10. Leonhardt, David, and Floyd Norris, "Fears Increase, but Consumers Keep Spending," *New York Times*, November 11, 2002.

11. www.cardweb.com.

12. "Debt the American Way," Yankelovich Partners survey for Lutheran Brotherhood, July 11, 2001.

13. Gordon, Marcy, "Bankruptcies Rise to Record Level," Associated Press, May 16, 2002.

14. U.S. Department of Commerce, Bureau of Economic Analysis, "Personal Saving as a Percentage of After Tax Investing," at www.bea.doc.gov.

15. "College Financial Fact Sheet," at www.upromise.com.

16. "Age and Personality Affect How Individuals Save for Retirement," Retirement Confidence Survey for the American Savings Education Council and the Employee Benefit Research Institute by Matthew Greenwald and Associates, February 27, 2002.

17. "Americans Prefer Money to Time, but Cherish Romance over Riches," *EPM Communications*, 18: 6 (March 17, 2000).

18. T.V. Turnoff Network at www.tvfa.org.

19. "Parents' Guilt + Kids' Costly Ways = Big Allowances," *Christian Science Monitor*, May 17, 2002.

20. Ibid.

21. Ibid.

22. Ibid.

23. Hayes, Constance, "Group Says Ads Manipulate Children with Psychology," *New York Times*, October 31, 1999.

24. "Debt as a Health Hazard," at www.cnnfn.com, April 13, 2000.

25. Farkas, Steve, Jean Johnson, and Ann Duffett, "A Lot Easier Said than Done: Parents Talk about Raising Children in Today's America," a report from *Public Agenda*, October 2002.

26. "College Students and Money: Majoring in Broke," Harris Interactive Survey for Lutheran Brotherhood, July 11, 2001.

27. "Minnesota Bankers Set Aside Day for Teaching; Teach Children to Save Day," at www.biz.yahoo.com, April 12, 2002.

Chapter EIGHT   Money See, Money Do

1. Yankelovich Partners national survey for Lutheran Brotherhood, July 2000.
2. Wechsler, Pat, "Hey Kid, Buy This," *BusinessWeek*, June 30, 1997.
3. NcNeal, James, *The Kids Market: Myths and Realities* (Ithaca, NY: Paramount Market Publishing, 1999), p. 78.
4. Ibid., p. 80.
5. Ibid.
6. Ibid., p. 81.

Chapter NINE   Your Money, Your Values

1. Center for a New American Dream at www.newdream.org.
2. *Bartlett's Familiar Quotations* (Boston: Little, Brown & Co., 1980), p. 63.
3. Ibid. p. 66.
4. Salkin, Jeffrey K., *Being God's Partner: How to Find the Hidden Link between Spirituality and Your Work* (Woodstock, VT: Jewish Lights Publishing, 1994), p. 42.
5. Ibid., p. 346.
6. Franklin, Benjamin, *Poor Richard's Almanack* (Mt. Vernon, NY: Peter Pauper Press, 1706–1790), p. 21.
7. *Bartlett's Familiar Quotations*, p. 557.
8. Ibid., p. 917.
9. Ibid., p. 66.
10. Franklin, *Poor Richard's Almanack*, p. 30.
11. *Bartlett's Familiar Quotations*, p. 565.
12. Center for a New American Dream at www.newdream.org.
13. New Revised Standard Version of the Bible, division of Christian Education of the National Council of the Churches of Christ in the United States of America (Nashville, TN: Thomas Nelson, 1989).

14. *Bartlett's Familiar Quotations*, p. 614.
15. Ibid., p. 796.
16. Dalai Lama and Howard C. Cutler, *The Art of Happiness: A Handbook for Living* (New York: Riverhead Books, 1998), p. 37.

Chapter FOURTEEN   Raising Your Child's Marketing IQ

1. Center for a New American Dream at www.newdream.org.
2. Gegax, T. Trent, "It's 4:00 P.M. Do You Know Where Your Children Are?" *Newsweek*, April 27, 1998.

Index

Index

DATE			
6/11/18			